THE
OVERCOMERS

WITNESS LEE

Living Stream Ministry
Anaheim, California

First Edition, October 1992.

ISBN 978-0-87083-674-9

Published by

Living Stream Ministry
2431 W. La Palma Ave., Anaheim, CA 92801 U.S.A.
P. O. Box 2121, Anaheim, CA 92814 U.S.A.

Printed in the United States of America

08 09 10 11 12 13 / 10 9 8 7 6 5 4

CONTENTS

PREFACE

This book is composed of messages given by Brother Witness Lee in Seattle, Washington on September 4-7, 1992.

CHAPTER ONE

GOD'S ECONOMY AND MAN'S FAILURE

Scripture Reading: 1 John 3:24; 4:13; Gen. 1:26-27; 2:7; 1 Thes. 5:23; 2 Cor. 5:17; Gal. 6:15; Gen. 13:16; 15:5; Rev. 12:5, 11; 14:1-5; Gen. 6:3a; 11:4-9; Jer. 2:13; 11:10; 2 Cor. 13:14; 1 John 3:8; Matt. 16:24; 1 John 2:15; Gal. 1:4; 6:14; Rev. 11:15

OUTLINE

I. God's economy:
   A. To be one with man—1 John 3:24; 4:13:
      1. Creating man in His image—Gen. 1:26-27.
      2. Making man of three parts—body, soul, and spirit—Gen. 2:7; 1 Thes. 5:23.
   B. To make man His organism:
      1. To be man's life and content.
      2. To express Himself in humanity.
   C. To have a new creation out of His old creation—2 Cor. 5:17; Gal. 6:15:
      1. To impart Himself into His old creation.
      2. To consummate this project in four ages in the old creation and through four peoples of His old creation:
         a. In the age before law through the race of Adam.
         b. In the age of law through the earthly descendants of the race of Abraham—Gen. 13:16.
         c. In the age of grace through the heavenly descendants of the race of Abraham—Gen. 15:5.
         d. In the age of the kingdom through the

overcomers of the races of Adam and of
Abraham—Rev. 12:5, 11; 14:1-5.

II. Man's failure:

A. The failure of the race of Adam in the age before
law:

1. Becoming flesh at the time of the deluge—Gen.
6:3a.

2. Becoming one with Satan at Babel—Gen. 11:4-9.

B. The failure of the earthly descendants of the race
of Abraham:

1. Forsaking God with His old covenant—Jer.
2:13; 11:10b.

2. Choosing Satan with his kingdom—Jer. 11:10a.

C. The failure of the heavenly descendants of the
race of Abraham:

1. Defeated in the enjoyment of the processed
Triune God—cf. 2 Cor. 13:14.

2. Corrupted by Satan through sin, self, the world,
and the religious world—1 John 3:8; Matt.
16:24; 1 John 2:15; Gal. 1:4; 6:14.

D. Christ calling the overcomers out of the heavenly
descendants of the race of Abraham for the age of
the kingdom:

1. To consummate God's economy.

2. To bring in the kingdom of Christ and of God—
Rev. 11:15.

This book concerning the overcomers is a continuation of our fellowship in the book entitled *The Satanic Chaos in the Old Creation and the Divine Economy for the New Creation.* The burden for the messages in this book can be expressed in the following four sets of statements concerning the overcomers from the book of Revelation:

Set 1:

To him who overcomes, I will give to eat of the tree of life, which is in the Paradise of God—Rev. 2:7.

To him who overcomes, I will give of the hidden manna—Rev. 2:17.

Set 2:

To him who overcomes, I will give a white stone, and upon the stone a new name written—Rev. 2:17.

He who overcomes, him I will make a pillar in the temple of My God—Rev. 3:12.

Set 3:

To him who hears My voice and opens the door, I will come in to him and dine with him and he with Me—Rev. 3:20.

He who overcomes, to him I will give to sit with Me on My throne, as I also overcame and sat with My Father on His throne—Rev. 3:21.

Set 4:

He who overcomes and he who keeps My works until the end, to him I will give authority over the nations—Rev. 2:26.

And he will shepherd them with an iron rod, as vessels of pottery are broken in pieces—Rev. 2:27.

The entire Scripture composed of sixty-six books concludes with two things: the overcomers and the New Jerusalem. These are the two main items revealed in the book of Revelation, the last book of the Bible. Revelation 1—20 gives us a complete record of the overcomers, and the New Jerusalem in Revelation 21—22 will be the issue, the coming out, the consummation, of the overcomers. The New Jerusalem will be manifested in two stages. The first stage will be in the millennium, the one-thousand-year kingdom. That will be the precursor of the New Jerusalem in the new heaven and new earth for eternity, the second stage of the New Jerusalem in the eternal age.

We may ask, "What is the New Jerusalem?" If we read Revelation thoroughly under the heavenly light, we can see that the New Jerusalem is the totality of the overcomers. The overcomers will be the New Jerusalem in the coming age, the age of the millennium, as the precursor to the New Jerusalem in eternity future. Only a relatively small part of the believers will be the overcomers. The majority of the believers—genuine, regenerated, blood-washed believers— will have been defeated. At the Lord's coming, He will take away only the overcomers, leaving the rest of the believers in another category because they will not have the maturity in His divine life. In the millennium the overcoming believers will be with Christ in the bright glory of the kingdom, whereas the defeated believers will suffer discipline in outer darkness (Matt. 8:12; 22:13; 25:30). This is so that they can be perfected for their maturity.

For any crop to become matured, that crop needs to go through a certain process. The process through which the immature believers will have to pass will not be pleasant but will be a period of discipline and punishment for one thousand years. Even though that will not be a pleasant process, it will complete God's eternal economy. All of these dear ones will be matured and perfected. After the thousand years, the Lord will clear up the entire universe through His judgment at the great white throne (Rev. 20:11-15). Then there will be the new heaven and the new earth with the New Jerusalem. The New Jerusalem in eternity will be greatly enlarged to include all the believers. By then all the believers will be overcomers (Rev. 21:7). The late ones will be later overcomers, whereas the overcomers in this age will be the earlier overcomers.

The earlier overcomers will be rewarded. The Lord will reward the overcomers in this age with what they are in Christ. They will enjoy their victory, but the defeated ones who were not ready will have nothing to enjoy as their reward.

Instead, the Lord will deal with them so that they can become matured and perfected. Eventually, the majority of the believers will enjoy what they are in Christ for eternity. We can prove this according to our experience. When we are victorious in the Lord, we enjoy our victory every day, but when we are defeated, the enjoyment of the Lord is gone. When we are victorious, the Lord is our enjoyment in what we are. What we would, could, and should enjoy in the Lord will be what we are. When people graduate from college, their graduation time is an enjoyment of what they are. They enjoy the fruit of their labor during their college years. Those who failed to make passing grades still have to come back to school so that they can graduate. This is the educational system's way.

This educational system is a wise way, but our God is wiser. He has a big operation in the universe. He selected millions of people, who were saved by grace. Grace is based upon mercy. Our salvation has nothing to do with what we are or with what we will be. God saved us and gave us so much. He gave us Himself, the divine life, the Holy Spirit, and Christ as His embodiment, the all-inclusive One. Because He gave us so much, we should be those who overcome. But regretfully many believers would not care for the Lord. They would care only for their eternal salvation. They would say, "As long as I am eternally saved and can go to heaven, I will be satisfied." They may be satisfied, but the Lord is not satisfied. Actually, whoever does not overcome in this age will not be satisfied in the next age. They will have nothing with which to be satisfied. Since we are Christians, we have to respond to the Lord's call to be overcomers.

We have pointed out that Revelation, the last book of the Bible, is a book concerning the overcomers (see *The Satanic Chaos in the Old Creation and the Divine Economy for the New Creation*, pp. 63-75). The last book of the Bible is nearly a closed book to many Christians. It seems that nobody understands what it is talking about. Revelation refers to the seven golden lampstands, the seven seals, the seven trumpets, and the seven bowls. Eventually, this book concludes with a mysterious city. According to Revelation 21:16, the city will be a square of twelve thousand stadia (a stadion equals about six hundred feet). The city is of pure gold and precious stones with gates of pearl (vv. 18-21). Many readers and teachers of the Bible do not see the significance of this mysterious city. Because many Bible teachers do not understand the book of Revelation, they basically avoid it in their teaching.

By the Lord's mercy, He has shown us that Revelation is a simple book. It was not written by a great scholar but by the apostle John, who was a fisherman on the Sea of Galilee. This fisherman surely did not have a theological mind. His writings are basically simple. In his Gospel, John opens in a simple way by saying, "In the beginning was the Word, and the Word was with God, and the Word was God" (John 1:1).

His final book, the book of Revelation, was also written in a very simple way, but from my youth I found it very difficult to understand. By reading it I realized that there must be something in it which is truly wonderful. Thank the Lord that gradually by His mercy, Revelation has become an open book to me. Once we see what is revealed in this book, we will see that it is very simple. The main subject of the first twenty chapters of the book of Revelation is the overcomers. Revelation 20 shows us that the overcoming martyrs will be resurrected to be the co-kings with Christ, the King, to enter into a city in which they will enjoy what they are in Christ (vv. 4-6).

An overcomer is someone who overcomes in every area of his daily life. The Lord Jesus is moving within us to live through us even in the way that we comb and cut our hair. If we do not follow Him in this matter, we will be defeated in having a worldly hair style. When the Lord says, "Don't comb your hair that way," we should respond, "Amen. Whatever You want, Lord Jesus." This is what it means to overcome. This means that we love Him more than our self, more than our soul-life. An overcomer knows and loves only Christ.

In a sense, the revelation concerning the overcomers is simple, but we may wonder why such a seemingly simple subject occupies the first twenty chapters of the book of Revelation. This is because there are different categories of overcomers. One category of overcomers is the martyrs of the Old Testament and the New Testament up to the time before the great tribulation. Revelation 6 unveils that these martyred saints are underneath the altar crying out, "How long, O Master, holy and true, will You not judge and avenge our blood on those who dwell on the earth?" (v. 10). The second category of overcomers is the man-child caught up to God and to His throne in Revelation 12:5. The third category of overcomers is the hundred and forty-four thousand living overcomers, the firstfruits, in Revelation 14:1-5. They will be raptured to the heavenly Mount Zion before the great tribulation. Those who are standing on the glassy sea in Revelation 15:2-4 are the fourth category of overcomers. These four categories of overcomers constitute the fifth category, which is the prepared bride in Revelation 19:7-9. Thank the Lord that He is able to make so many of His believers overcomers. We need twenty chapters of the book of Revelation to show us how the believers are made overcomers by the Lord's abounding and sufficient grace.

The last two chapters of Revelation unveil the New Jerusalem in the new heaven and the new earth for eternity. That will be the totality of all the believers throughout all the generations of the Old Testament and the New Testament. By then all of God's chosen and redeemed people will have been made overcomers. This gives us an overview of the book of Revelation.

The Bible as a whole is the history of God. Many people have had histories, or biographies, written about them. When I finished writing the biography of Brother Watchman Nee (entitled *Watchman Nee: A Seer of the Divine Revelation in the Present Age*), I considered that God also has a biography, a history. The Bible is the best history of God. The Old Testament is the history of God with man, and the New Testament is the history of God in continuation within man. In the Old Testament, God was only with man. He did not get into man until He became incarnated. Incarnation was God entering into man. The first chapter of the New Testament in the Gospel of Matthew gives us a record of how God entered into man. From that day the God with man became the very God within man.

Thank God that we are saved, regenerated, blood-washed, and Spirit-filled Christians with God in us! If someone asks us who we are, we might say, "I am a Christian." A Christian is a believer in Christ. But who are you as a believer in Christ? The top answer is—"I am God within me." We believers are "God in us." The church is God in a group of human beings. This does not mean that we are God in His Godhead but that we have God within us as our life, nature, element, and essence. To say that we are "God in us" means that we are a part of God's history. The Bible is the history of God with man in the Old Testament and then of God within man in the New Testament.

I. GOD'S ECONOMY

Our God has an eternal economy (Eph. 1:10; 3:9; 1 Tim. 1:4). *Economy* means plan. God has an eternal plan. He planned in eternity past to do something, and this plan was made by Himself according to His heart's desire, according to His good pleasure, to carry out His intention. God has a heart's desire, and He has to do something to work out what He desires. God has an eternal plan, an eternal economy, with an intention to do something.

A. To Be One with Man

The great God, who is very active and living, has an intention to be one with man. This may seem very simple, but this most simple thing is the most mysterious thing. Medical doctors have been studying the human body for many years, but they still cannot fully comprehend all of its mysteries. One doctor told me that after studying the human body, one cannot deny that there must be an almighty Being in the universe. Otherwise, the wonderful human body could not have come into existence. The human body seems to be simple, but this simple thing is wonderful. God's economy to be one with man also may seem simple, but such a simple thing is the most wonderful thing.

Because we have believed into Christ, God is one with us.

Do not forget that this is the very God who is one with us! The very God is in our spirit as a Spirit (2 Tim. 4:22; 2 Cor. 3:17). The Bible says that God indwells us and we indwell Him (1 John 3:24; 4:13). That means God is in us and we are in Him. We and God indwell each other. Theologians came up with the word *coinherence* to describe this mutual indwelling. The eternal God as the eternal life is in us and we are in the eternal God. Who can explain the fact that God and man coinhere? This is altogether wonderful!

1. Creating Man in His Image

Because God wanted to indwell man, He created man in His own image (Gen. 1:26-27). This identifies man with God outwardly. Outwardly, we look like God. Darwin said that we are descendants of monkeys, but this is nonsense. We are not descendants of monkeys, but we are men who were created in the image of God. Among the millions of items of God's creation, nothing can compare with man. All the other living things are after their kind, but man is after God's kind. This is because man bears God's image; he resembles God.

2. Making Man of Three Parts— Body, Soul, and Spirit

Man bears God's image so that he can be a container to contain God, that is, a vessel to be filled with God. This is why God made man in three parts—body, soul, and spirit (Gen. 2:7; 1 Thes. 5:23). Man was made as a container to receive God, and the container must be in the form of its contents. God made us with a spirit to receive Him, with a mind to understand Him, with a heart to love Him, and with a body to express Him. Thus, we have an organ to receive God, an organ to understand Him, an organ to love Him, and an organ, an outer vessel, to express Him. In this way, God can be one with us and we can be one with Him.

B. To Make Man His Organism

God wanted to be one with man to make man His organism. The spiritual, abstract, and mysterious God wants to have an organism. Our physical body is an organism. God wants to have a Body, that is, the Body of Christ, as His organism.

God makes man His organism by being man's life and content to express Himself in humanity. Jesus was God in humanity. He was a real man, and God was living in Him, through Him, and out of Him. He was a man who expressed God in all of God's attributes in His humanity. Jesus is so lovable and so beautiful because He is a man, but God lives in Him. God lives in Him with all of God's attributes for the expression of God through humanity.

We believers as the followers of Jesus are also men living God, expressing God, and letting God live out through us in our humanity. We Christians do not live according to our wisdom or our cleverness. We live God. The unbelievers may think that we are foolish, but actually we are the wisest people. On the other hand, the apostle Paul said that "we are fools because of Christ" (1 Cor. 4:10). We are foolish in others' eyes because we forsake our human wisdom for the sake of Christ. We are human yet we live God. We express God's attributes through our human virtues.

C. To Have a New Creation
out of His Old Creation

God created the universe and man. This is His old creation. However, His intention is not to have an old creation. He intends to have a new creation (2 Cor. 5:17; Gal. 6:15).

1. To Impart Himself into His Old Creation

In order to have a new creation, God imparts Himself into His old creation. The old creation does not have God within it. It does not have God's life or God's nature, but the new creation, constituted of the believers, who are born again of God, does (John 1:13; 3:15; 2 Pet. 1:4). Hence, the believers are a new creation (Gal. 6:15), not according to the old nature of the flesh but according to the new nature of the divine life.

Before we were regenerated, we were the old creation without God in us, but today we are happy because we have God within us. He is our joy. The Bible says that we should always rejoice (1 Thes. 5:16; Phil. 4:4). Human life, however, is full of suffering and anxiety. After passing through so much suffering, Job indicated that he wished he had not been born (Job 3:1-13). How can we not be anxious about anything? This is impossible in ourselves. We can be free from anxiety only when we are living in God. God is our dwelling place. Moses said, "Lord, thou hast been our dwelling place in all generations" (Psa. 90:1). God is our eternal house for us to dwell in. He is our dwelling place, and we are His dwelling place (1 Cor. 3:16; Eph. 2:22). We abide in Him and He abides in us. This mutual abode is the new creation, and this new creation is God's intention.

2. To Consummate This Project in Four Ages in the Old Creation and through Four Peoples of His Old Creation

God's eternal economy is for Him to be one with man, making man His organism so that He can have a new creation out of the old creation. This is not a simple project. God consummates this project in four ages in the old creation and through four peoples of His old creation.

According to the Bible, there are four ages in the old creation—the age before law, the age of law, the age of grace, and the age of the kingdom. God worked in the first age, the age before law, through the race of Adam, from Adam to Moses. He continued to work in the second age, the age of law, from Moses to Christ's first coming, through the earthly descendants of the race of Abraham (Gen. 13:16). He goes on in the third age, the age of grace, which is the church age, from Christ's first coming to His second coming, through the heavenly descendants of the race of Abraham (Gen. 15:5). Then He will work to consummate His project to have a new creation in the fourth age, the last age, the age of the kingdom of one thousand years, through the overcomers of the races of Adam and Abraham (Rev. 12:5, 11; 14:1-5). God uses these four ages to consummate His economy.

This divine project takes God thousands of years to accomplish. From Adam to Abraham was two thousand years, from Abraham to Christ was two thousand years, and from

Christ to today is almost two thousand years. Thus, almost six thousand years have passed since the time of Adam. Eventually, there will be the millennial kingdom, the kingdom of one thousand years. We can see from this that it takes God thousands of years to accomplish the project of His economy to be one with man, making man His organism so that man can become His new creation with Himself as the life content.

Today we are in the age of grace under the process of God's project to have a new creation. Any thoughtful person desires to know what the meaning of human life is. Solomon said in Ecclesiastes that everything under the sun is vanity of vanities (1:2-3). But thank the Lord that we are in His intention and that we know the meaning of human life. God chose us before the foundation of the world (Eph. 1:4) and called us in time to carry out His eternal economy to have a new creation. God has a purpose, a project, and we are in the process of His project day by day. I hope that eventually I can be counted by Him as one of the overcomers. My goal is eventually to be an overcomer.

II. MAN'S FAILURE

God will take at least seven thousand years to finish His project of gaining the new creation out of the old creation. He takes four ages to do this because the human race failed God.

A. The Failure of the Race of Adam in the Age before Law

God created Adam, which means that He chose Adam with his descendants to be the very means for Him to bring forth the new creation. Eventually, however, the Adamic race became flesh at the time of the deluge (Gen. 6:3a). At the time of the flood, man had become totally sinful and ugly in the sight of God. Later, the Adamic race became one with Satan at Babel (Gen. 11:4-9). Man became satanic. Then God came in to choose Abraham so that He could have a new race, a called race.

B. The Failure of the Earthly Descendants of the Race of Abraham

But even the new race, the called race, the earthly descendants of the race of Abraham, became a failure. They forsook God with His old covenant (Jer. 2:13; 11:10b), choosing Satan with his kingdom (11:10a).

C. The Failure of the Heavenly Descendants of the Race of Abraham

Abraham has two kinds of descendants. One kind is signified by the dust. Genesis 13:16 tells us that the descendants of Abraham were likened to the dust of the earth. These are his earthly descendants, the Jews according to the flesh. The second category of Abraham's descendants, according to Genesis 15:5, are likened to the stars of heaven. These are the New Testament believers, the spiritual, heavenly descendants of Abraham. Galatians 6:16 says that we, the New Testament believers, are the spiritual Israel of God.

The heavenly descendants of Abraham also become a failure. They become defeated in the enjoyment of the processed Triune God (cf. 2 Cor. 13:14) and corrupted by Satan through sin, self, the world, and the religious world (1 John 3:8; Matt. 16:24; 1 John 2:15; Gal. 1:4; 6:14). The later Epistles of Paul and the epistles to the seven churches in Revelation 2 and 3 show that by the end of the first century, the church had become degraded. Thus, the created race became a failure, the chosen race as the earthly descendants of Abraham became a failure, and the heavenly descendants of Abraham also became a failure. This is why the Lord Jesus came in the book of Revelation to call for overcomers. He calls for the overcomers seven times in His epistles to the seven churches in Revelation 2 and 3 (2:7, 11, 17, 26-28; 3:5, 12, 20-21). He is calling us, the believers, the heavenly stars and the heavenly descendants of Abraham, to be the overcomers.

With the race of Adam, God suffered a loss. With Abraham's descendants of dust, God suffered a loss. With Abraham's heavenly descendants, God also suffered a loss. But with the last group of people, the overcomers, God gains the victory. In the last book of the Bible, Revelation, we see that Christ has gained a group of overcomers, and this group eventually becomes a big success to God.

D. Christ Calling the Overcomers out of the Heavenly Descendants of the Race of Abraham for the Age of the Kingdom

Christ calls the overcomers out of the heavenly descendants of the race of Abraham for the age of the kingdom to consummate God's economy and to bring in the kingdom of Christ and of God (Rev. 11:15). Some Christians today are sighing and groaning about the pitiful and defeated situation of the church. Apparently, this is right, but hiddenly throughout the centuries, there have been groups of overcomers. I believe that among us there are some overcomers. I can testify from the depths of my being that some of the saints with whom I served for many years are overcomers. We should not think that the church is wholly defeated. Apparently, it is defeated; actually, it is not. There is a group of saints who are standing with the Caller, Christ, to be His overcomers.

The overcomers consummate God's economy and eventually bring in God's kingdom. As overcomers, we do not live ourselves. We are living God. While we are living God, we are conquering all kinds of circumstances. In 1 Corinthians, Paul charged the saints to be full-grown men and to be strong (16:13). Paul's word was given not only to the brothers but also to the sisters at Corinth. We all need to be such strong, full-grown men. We should forget about ourselves because God is in us. We have to overcome, to conquer, all our circumstances. Then we have to subdue our environment. This is to bring in and spread God's dominion, which is to bring in God's kingdom. It is wrong to wait passively for God's kingdom to come. God needs a number of overcomers to conquer the circumstances and to subdue the environment so that His dominion will be brought in and spread for the bringing in of His kingdom.

CHAPTER TWO

TO OVERCOME THE LEAVING
OF THE FIRST LOVE

Scripture Reading: Rev. 2:1-7; 12:17b; 20:4, 6; 1 John 4:8, 16; John 3:16; 1 John 4:9; Rom. 5:5; 2 Cor. 13:14; Eph. 2:4-5; John 1:12-13; 3:3-6, 29-30; Rev. 19:7; 21:2, 7; Eph. 5:25; Rev. 21:9; Rom. 8:35-39; 2 Cor. 5:14-15; Rom. 14:7-9; Rev. 2:10; 12:11; 22:17; Jer. 2:2; 31:3

OUTLINE

I. In a church:
   A. Being orderly and formal—Rev. 2:2-3.
   B. But having left the first love—v. 4.
II. To overcome the leaving of the first love—v. 5a:
   A. The first love—the best love:
      1. The love which is God Himself—1 John 4:8, 16:
         a. To give His only begotten Son to us as our portion—John 3:16.
         b. To send His Son into the world that we might have life and live through Him—1 John 4:9.
         c. To be poured out in our hearts through the Holy Spirit—Rom. 5:5.
         d. To be the source for our enjoyment of the dispensing of the Triune God—2 Cor. 13:14.
      2. As the Father's love in life to regenerate us that we may become His children—Eph. 2:4-5; John 1:12-13.
      3. God's regenerated children become the members of Christ to constitute the Body of Christ, the

bride of Christ, as His increase for Him to
love—John 3:3-6, 29-30; Rev. 19:7; 21:2, 7.
  4. Christ as the Husband loves the church as His
     wife with the Father's love as the love of affec-
     tion—Eph. 5:25; Rev. 21:9; Rom. 8:35, 39:
     a. Christ's love of affection constrains us to
        live and to die for Him—2 Cor. 5:14-15; Rom.
        14:7-9.
     b. Christ's love makes the believers martyrs
        for Him—Rev. 2:10; 12:11; Rom. 8:35-37.
  B. To recover the first love is to recover the bridal
     love, the eternal love, for the Lord—Rev. 22:17;
     cf. Jer. 2:2; 31:3.
  C. To repent and do the first works.
III. To maintain the eating of Christ as the tree of
     life—Rev. 2:7:
  A. To continue the enjoyment of the life supply of
     Christ.
  B. In the present church life of the Paradise of God.
IV. To shine forth the divine light as the lampstand—
     cf. v. 5b:
  A. Corporately versus individualistically.
  B. In the dark night of the church age.
 V. To keep the testimony of Jesus as the shining of the
     lampstand in their locality—Rev. 12:17b:
  A. Testifying Christ's person as God and as man.
  B. Testifying Christ's human living, crucifixion,
     resurrection, ascension, descension, and second
     appearing.
  C. In our daily life.
VI. To be rewarded—Rev. 2:7:
  A. To participate in full in the enjoyment of the rich
     life supply of Christ as the embodiment of the
     processed and consummated Triune God.
  B. In the New Jerusalem in its freshness as the
     Paradise of God for one thousand years—Rev.
     20:4, 6.

In the first chapter we saw God's economy and man's failure. In this chapter we want to begin to fellowship concerning all of the things which we need to overcome.

OVERCOMING JUDAISM, CATHOLICISM, AND PROTESTANTISM

In the seven epistles to the churches in Revelation 2 and 3, there is not much concerning the overcoming of sin, self, and the world. Instead the Lord stresses that we need to overcome three things, which I call three "isms." Every "ism" refers to a religion. Throughout human history and even until today there have been three main religions, three "isms"—Judaism, Catholicism, and Protestantism.

In the epistle to the church in Smyrna, the Lord referred to the "synagogue of Satan" (Rev. 2:9). The synagogue is a strong sign of Judaism. Since the time that the Jews lost their temple and were scattered throughout the whole world, they began to worship God in places other than the temple. According to Deuteronomy 12, no one has the right to worship God anywhere except in the place chosen by God, the place where His temple was built. The temple could be built on this earth only in the place, in the very spot, which God had chosen. Jerusalem was the spot where the temple was built, but the Roman prince Titus destroyed that temple, not leaving one stone upon another stone (Matt. 24:2). The temple with the city of Jerusalem was thoroughly devastated in A.D. 70. Since then all the scattered Jews have worshipped God in their synagogues. Thus, the synagogues are strong signs of the Jewish religion. The Jews even refer to their synagogues as temples, but they are not the temple. Apparently those in the synagogue were worshipping God, yet the Lord Jesus said that the synagogues were not of God but of Satan. Judaism has been greatly usurped and utilized by Satan to damage God's interest on this earth and to persecute and martyr many faithful ones (see Rev. 2:9, note 9[5]—Recovery Version).

In the fourth epistle, to Thyatira, we see another "ism," Catholicism. In this epistle the Lord refers to a woman by the name of Jezebel (Rev. 2:20). In Matthew 13 He speaks of a woman who mixed leaven with three measures of meal to thoroughly leaven it (v. 33). This woman in Matthew 13 is Jezebel in Revelation 2, signifying Catholicism.

We can see Protestantism in the fifth epistle, to the church in Sardis. The Lord told those in Sardis that they had a name that they were living, but actually they were dead (Rev. 3:1). Protestant Christianity is dead and dying. Some may consider the reformed Protestant Church to be living, but the Lord said that she is dead. Hence, she needs the living Spirit and the shining stars (v. 1).

Later in this book we will see that these three "isms"— Judaism, Catholicism, and Protestantism—are the damaging factors on this earth to interrupt and to annul God's interest. In the seven epistles to the seven churches, what the Lord charges us to overcome is mainly these three "isms." These three religions were invented according to and based upon God's holy Word, but all of them have deviated from God's holy Word to become something different in nature from the church revealed in the holy Word. We all have to respond to the Lord's charge to overcome these three religions.

Now we need to consider the history behind the formation of these three religions. In Genesis God created man in His own image and in three parts with a spirit which is full of capacity to contact God, to receive God, and to retain God (1:26; 2:7). Then God placed man before the tree of life with the intention that man would receive Him as life (2:9). But right away Satan came in, seducing Adam to take the wrong tree. That tree is the tree of death, the tree of the knowledge of good and evil. That devastated the very man whom God had created for His purpose.

Then this man, a corporate man which we call mankind, became altogether the flesh, full of lusts. This is clearly unveiled in Genesis 6 (vv. 3, 5-6). God could not tolerate such an evil world any longer, so He decided to judge the world by the flood. He charged Noah to make an ark for his and his family's salvation from the damage of Satan (vv. 11-14). Then Noah became a new beginning for God. But later the descendants of Noah became one with Satan at Babel, which was full of idols (Gen. 11:1-9). Thus, the man whom God had created failed utterly in fulfilling God's purpose, becoming one with God's enemy.

Then God came in to call another man by the name of Abraham. Through Abraham God gained a people whom He brought out of Egypt to Mount Sinai. There God gave them the law, the Pentateuch, through Moses. We may say that this was the origin of Judaism, the origin of the Jewish religion. It was founded absolutely according to God's holy Word, but gradually the children of Israel became corrupted and rotten because they forsook God Himself as their source, the fountain of living waters. In Jeremiah 2:13, Jehovah said, "For My people have committed two evils: / They have forsaken Me, / The fountain of living waters, / To hew out for themselves cisterns, / Broken cisterns, / Which hold no water." All the idols are broken cisterns which cannot retain water. The two evils are forsaking God and joining with Satan in worshipping idols. These are the two evils that resulted in the failure of the people of Israel, who were the descendants of Abraham in an earthly sense as the dust of the earth (Gen. 13:16). God sent the Babylonians to come to devastate Jerusalem and the temple and carry the people away into captivity in 606 B.C. Of course, God brought a remnant of them back after seventy years to rebuild the temple (Jer. 29:10), but that recovery did not last too long.

The four Gospels show us how evil the Jewish people had become by the time that the Lord Jesus came. The entire holy land was full of demons. Wherever the Lord Jesus went, He confronted demons. The Lord Jesus appeared to the people of Israel as their Shepherd to shepherd them and even as their Savior to rescue them, but they totally rejected Him.

In Matthew 23 the Lord Jesus lamented over them and told them, "Behold, your house is left to you desolate" (v. 38). This indicated that they would be rejected by the Triune God. The Lord said that from that day the temple, which was the house of God, would no longer be the house of God, but "your house." Then when the disciples came to Him to show Him the buildings of the temple, He said to them, "Do you not see all these things? Truly I say to you, There shall by no means be left here a stone upon a stone, which shall not be thrown down" (24:2). The Lord was predicting that the temple with the city of Jerusalem would be devastated, not leaving one stone upon another stone. This was fulfilled in A.D. 70 when Titus and the Roman army destroyed Jerusalem, shortly after the Lord had ascended to the heavens. That destruction was an unprecedented event in history. Josephus, the Jewish historian, spoke of the cruelty and slaughter inflicted upon the inhabitants of Jerusalem by the Roman army.

After this destruction by Titus, the Jews were scattered all over the earth. Since that time, Hosea tells us that the Jewish people have been "without king and without prince and without sacrifice and without pillar and without ephod and teraphim" (3:4). Among the Jews for nearly twenty centuries, there have been no kings, no princes, no prophets, no priests, and no sacrifices, because there have been no temple and no altar to receive the sacrifices. Hosea predicted that this time of desolation would last two days, or two thousand years (6:1-2). According to history, this period of two thousand years should begin from Titus' destruction of Jerusalem in A.D. 70. From that day until today among the Jews, there have been no kings, no princes, no priests, no prophets, and no sacrifices; nor have there been any idols among the Jews since that time. The Jewish people invented their way of synagogues to worship God, but the Lord referred to the synagogue as a synagogue of Satan.

Later, the church came into existence, but it was not too long before the church became worldly, married to the world. That worldly church eventually became the Roman Catholic Church at the end of the sixth century when the papal system was established and the pope was commonly recognized. This Roman Church is typified by the woman Jezebel in Revelation 2:20.

Now I would like us to read Revelation 17:16: "And the ten horns which you saw and the beast, these will hate the harlot and will make her desolate and naked and will eat her flesh and burn her utterly with fire." This verse was written at the end of the first century in approximately A.D. 90, but most Christians do not know that there is such a verse in the Bible. They do not know that the Lord Jesus sounded the trumpet seven times in Revelation for us to overcome, nor do they know what to overcome. My burden is for us to see what we need to overcome, and Revelation 17:16 will help us to see this. The ten horns in this verse are the ten kings (v. 12), and the beast is Antichrist (Rev. 13:1-10). The harlot in Revelation 17 is the Roman Catholic Church (vv. 1-6). Antichrist is the head, and the ten kings belong to Antichrist, so they all agree to do one thing. They will hate the Roman Catholic Church and make her desolate and naked and will eat her flesh and will burn her utterly with fire. This will be the end of the Roman Catholic Church.

Antichrist will be empowered to be the last Caesar of the revived Roman Empire (see Rev. 17:10-11, notes 10[1] and 11[1]— Recovery Version), and he will make a covenant with Israel for the last seven years of this age, but after three and a half years he will break this covenant (Dan. 9:27). He will rebel against God and persecute any kind of religion (2 Thes. 2:3-4). He will not allow anyone to worship anything or anyone but himself. Then with the ten kings under him he will desolate and burn the Roman Catholic Church. Revelation 17:16 makes us clear that at the beginning of the great tribulation of three and a half years, the Roman Catholic Church will be desolated and burned by Antichrist. This is not a spiritual burning but a physical burning. Not many know that there is such a verse in Revelation.

Recent statistics say that the Roman Catholic Church has fifty-five million members in the United States, nearly half of all those in Christianity. This shows us that millions have been deceived by Catholicism. They do not realize that what they are in is something false and even satanic and devilish. The main thing in Revelation 17 is that the Lord has fixed a day for Antichrist and his ten kings to desolate and burn the Roman Catholic Church. Revelation 2:24 tells us that the deep things of Satan are within this apostate church. This is satanic and devilish. The Lord will tolerate this up to the beginning of the great tribulation when the Roman Catholic Church will be terminated by Antichrist.

Now we have to consider today's Protestant churches in the light of the divine revelation. The most significant thing

in the Protestant churches is that they are full of nominal
Christians, false Christians. In Matthew 13 the Lord uses
the tares to signify the false Christians. Among the fifty-five
million Catholics and sixty-five million Protestants in the
United States, how many are real believers and how many are
false ones? In the true church, all are saved, blood-washed,
Spirit-regenerated believers. Many in the Protestant churches
today, however, are not genuine believers in Christ; instead,
they are tares, false Christians. Concerning the destiny of
the tares, the Lord said that they would be collected and cast
into the lake of fire at the consummation of this age (Matt.
13:30, 40-42).

In today's Christendom there are the wheat, the real
believers, and the tares, the false ones. While the tares and the
wheat are growing together, they are difficult to differentiate.
It is impossible to distinguish wheat from tares until the fruit
is produced. The wheat brings forth yellow fruit, and the
tares bring forth something black. Often it is hard to discern
who is a real Christian and who is a false one in today's
Christendom. Concerning the wheat and the tares, the Lord
said, "Let both grow together until the harvest, and at the
time of the harvest I will say to the reapers, Collect first
the tares and bind them into bundles to burn them up, but
the wheat gather into my barn" (Matt. 13:30). This will take
place when the Lord Jesus comes back at the end of the great
tribulation. The Lord will send the angels to bind all the false
Christians into bundles, and they will be cast into the lake of
fire (Matt. 13:42). In this way the Lord Jesus will clear up the
mixture.

At the beginning of the great tribulation, Antichrist with
the ten kings will devastate and burn the Roman Catholic
Church. Then after three and a half years, at the end of the
great tribulation, the Lord Jesus will come back and send His
angels to bind all the false Christians and throw them into
the lake of fire. These are the two endings of the two "isms,"
Catholicism and Protestantism. This is not according to my
idea or teaching, but this is the divine revelation, showing us
how these two "isms," Catholicism and Protestantism, will
be ended. First, Catholicism will be ended by Antichrist in the

middle of the last seven years of this age, at the beginning of the great tribulation. Then Protestantism will be cleared up by the Lord at His coming back. The biggest devastation to Christianity is the tares. This is why many people in the world condemn Christianity. When you try to talk to them about Christ, they think that you are trying to get them to accept Christianity. They see the evils and hypocrisy in Christianity. But in the Lord's recovery today we do not preach Christianity. We preach Christ. We desire only Christ, not any "anity." We do not preach any religion. We preach only a living person, and this living person is Christ as the very God who became a man and died on the cross for us. We preach this One so that people will believe into Him for their salvation. We are not convincing others to believe and receive Christianity. We are telling people that they need Christ, the person.

We need to be clear about these three "isms" on the earth today—Judaism, Catholicism, and Protestantism. Judaism presently has about five million members in the United States. The United States has a population of about two hundred thirty million people, and over half of these are professing Christians in Catholicism and Protestantism. We need to realize that both Catholicism and Protestantism are condemned by God. One will be burned by fire on this earth, and the "tares" of the other will be burned by fire in the lake of fire. Therefore, we have to overcome the Jewish religion, the Catholic Church, and the Protestant churches.

Of course, there are a good number of saved, genuine believers in both the Catholic Church and the Protestant churches. But there is a mixture of saved ones and unsaved ones. Today in both the Catholic Church and the Protestant churches, many are real believers. This is why the Lord sounded the call for His people to come out of Babylon (Rev. 18:4). This calling tells us that the Lord does not feel good about His people remaining in Catholicism and Protestant-ism. This also shows that even the Lord Jesus admitted that there are real Christians in both the Catholic Church and the Protestant churches. Otherwise, He would not call His people to come out of Babylon.

Today the people of God need to overcome the three "isms" and come back to a unique, living, divine and human Person. He is our Savior, our God, our Redeemer, our Lord, and our Master, and He has nothing to do with any "anity." He has nothing to do with any religion.

TO OVERCOME THE LEAVING OF THE FIRST LOVE

The Lord charges us to overcome all kinds of religion, and in these seven epistles He also charges us to overcome some other matters. The first thing we are charged to overcome is the leaving, the missing, the losing, of the first love (Rev. 2:4-5a). Many in Catholicism are absolutely for the Catholic Church, but they do not love the Lord or His holy Word. They do not say, "The Bible says...." Instead, they say, "The pope says..." or "The church says...." When they say "the church," they mean the Catholic Church. This is why the Lord Jesus in Revelation 2 says that Jezebel calls herself a prophetess and teaches and leads His slaves astray (v. 20). This indicates that the Roman Catholic Church is a self-appointed prophetess, one who presumes to be authorized by God to speak for God. Those who are loyal Catholics respect only what the pope says, what the church says. They do not care for what the Bible says. This indicates that they do not have any love given to the Lord.

If we love someone, we surely want to hear his voice, his word. On the other hand, if we do not love a person, we do not want to hear his voice, his word. A number of Catholics are like this toward the Lord. They have Christ in name, but they do not have any personal affection or loving element within them toward Christ. It is also like this with the tares in Protestantism, who are not saved. They have no element of love toward the Lord personally.

I must testify that I love the Lord. I received the Lord sixty-seven years ago in 1925. After all of these years, I feel that the Lord is still so intimate to me and that I am so close to Him. I do not care for any religion. I care for this dear One, this living One. Whenever I mention His name, I am happy. When we wake up in the morning, the first thing we should do is say, "O Lord Jesus. O Lord Jesus." It is better to add, "I love You." We should say, "O Lord Jesus, I love You. O Lord Jesus, I love You." How intimate, how sweet, and how affectionate this is!

Our God, our Christ, our Lord, is not only loving but also very affectionate. He is full of affection. God has "fallen in love" with us, His chosen and redeemed people. If you say, "O Lord Jesus, I love You," right away you will fall in love with Him. Quite often I would not do some things, not merely because they are not right or because I fear God but because I love Him. I would say, "Lord Jesus, I love You, so I cannot do this." I just cannot do certain things, because I love Him.

We need to overcome the loss of the first love. The church in Ephesus was a good church. It was an orderly church and a formal church (Rev. 2:2-3). Surely we would like such a church, but such an orderly church had left the first love (v. 4). The Greek word for *first* is the same as that translated *best* in Luke 15:22. Our first love toward the Lord must be the best love for Him. When the prodigal son in Luke 15 came back home, the father told the servants to bring the *best* robe. The *best* here is the first.

Now I would like us to consider what the first love is. Many Christians think that the first love is the love with which we loved the Lord Jesus when we were saved. I would not say that this is wrong, but it is not adequate. The first love which is the best love is much more than this.

The first love is the love which is God Himself. In the Bible we are told that God is love (1 John 4:8, 16). In the whole universe, only God is love. The Lord charges the husbands to love their wives. But it is impossible for the husbands to love their wives in themselves because we are not love. There is only one Person who is love—God.

God is not only the best but also the first. In the whole universe, God is first. Genesis 1:1 says, "In the beginning God...." This is the opening of the Bible. God is the beginning. God is the first. Colossians tells us that our Christ must have the first place. He must have the preeminence (1:18b). Christ must be the first. What is it to recover the first love? To recover the first love is to consider the Lord Jesus as the first in everything. If we make Christ everything in our life, that means we have overcome the loss of the first love.

We need to consider our situation. Is Christ the first in everything with us? The first item we have to overcome is the loss of Christ as the first, as the best, as the real love. The failure of Israel was that they forsook God, the fountain of living waters, and the degradation of the church is the leaving of the first love. Actually, to leave the first love is just to leave Christ, not taking Him as the first in everything.

Christ should be first not only in big things but also in small things. When the brothers buy a necktie, they should give Christ the first place. If I wore a certain kind of tie in a very worldly style, I would not be able to speak for the Lord in my ministry. Even for the sake of my conscience, I cannot wear certain styles of ties. The sisters should give Christ the first place in the way that they style their hair. If the sisters give Christ the preeminence in the way that they style their hair, this means that they are taking Him as their first love. Sisters who have a worldly hair style do not have Christ as their first love. They are not giving Him the preeminence. We should give Christ the preeminence in the way that we dress and the way that we style our hair. When we give Christ the preeminence in everything, this is to recover the loss of the first love.

Some think that the first love was our love for the Lord at the beginning of our Christian life when we were saved. But when I was saved, although I was very grateful to the Lord, I did not have such a strong heart to love Christ as I do today. Sixty-seven years ago I was saved and I loved the Lord Jesus, but not as much as I do today. Thus, the first love must be to have God, Christ, the Lord, our Master, as the first One in everything.

At times when I am getting dressed, I talk to the Lord by saying, "Lord, do You like this shirt? Do You like this pair of shoes?" Such a talk is very intimate with the Lord as the first love. To recover the first love is to give Him the preeminence in great things as well as in small things. The husbands should give Christ the preeminence in the way that they talk to their wives. We need to ask the Lord to forgive us for all the things in which we do not give Him the preeminence. If we love the Lord Jesus in such a way and to such an extent, we will never stay in the three "isms." We will never remain in any religion. We will love all the Christians, but we will hate any "anity." We should love all the Christians, but we should hate the religions in which they are. Because the Lord hates these "isms," we also should hate them. We should hate what the Lord hates (cf. Rev. 2:6).

The Lord said to let the wheat and the tares grow together until the harvest. Then when He comes back, the first thing He will do is to send angels to bind up the tares in bundles and throw them into the lake of fire. The sons of the kingdom, the wheat, constitute the kingdom, whereas the sons of the evil one, the tares, have formed the outward appearance of the kingdom, which is today's Christendom. The Lord hates this outward appearance, so we must overcome it.

We also need to overcome in the kind of ties we wear, in the way that we style our hair, and in all of the small things. In all things we should give the preeminence to Christ. If we do this, our Christian life will be different, and our feeling will be different. Throughout the day, we will be happy in the Lord. When we are joyful in and with the Lord, everything is pleasant. On the other hand, when we are not joyful in the Lord and with the Lord, everything is unpleasant. The enjoyment of the Lord as grace is with those who love Him (Eph. 6:24). Thus, the first thing we have to overcome is the leaving of the first love. The leaving of the first love is the source of and main reason for the failure of the church throughout the ages.

TO MAINTAIN THE EATING OF CHRIST
AS THE TREE OF LIFE

In such a good, orderly, and formal church like the church in Ephesus, we need to first overcome the loss of the first love. The second thing we need is to maintain the eating of Christ as the tree of life. It is in the epistle to the Ephesians that the Lord says, "To him who overcomes, to him I will give to eat of the tree of life, which is in the Paradise of God" (Rev. 2:7).

The Lord Jesus charged us to overcome the leaving of the first love and to maintain the eating of Christ as the tree of life. If we give the preeminence to Christ in everything and enjoy Him as the tree of life every day, we will be marvelous, overcoming Christians. When we enjoy Christ as the tree of life, we have the Paradise of God. The tree of life is first seen in Genesis in the garden of Eden. That garden of Eden was the paradise of God at that time. Today our paradise is the church life.

I have been in the church life for sixty years, starting from 1932, so I have much church life experience. If you do not give the preeminence to the Lord or enjoy the Lord, even for a month, the church life may become an unpleasant place to you. Of course, you might not say this, but deep within you would think that there is not much good in the church life. Then the church is altogether no longer a paradise to you. But when you overcome the loss of the first love and maintain your eating of Christ, your enjoying of the Lord, right away the church life becomes paradise to you. Thus, our sensation and our attitude toward the church depend upon our situation. If we give the Lord the preeminence in everything and enjoy Him as the tree of life throughout the day, right away the church, regardless of its condition, becomes paradise to us. This is why the Lord says that we have to eat the tree of life in the Paradise of God.

Of course, the Paradise of God in Revelation 2:7 actually refers to the New Jerusalem in the thousand-year kingdom. If we enjoy the Lord in this age, we will be rewarded with the eating of the tree of life, Christ Himself, in the New Jerusalem as the Paradise of God in the thousand-year kingdom. We need to continue in the enjoyment of the life supply of Christ in the present church life so that we can be rewarded with the enjoyment of Christ as the tree of life in the Paradise of God, the New Jerusalem, in the millennial kingdom. In the New Jerusalem in its freshness as the Paradise of God, we will participate in full in the enjoyment of the rich life supply of Christ as the embodiment of the processed and consummated Triune God.

TO SHINE FORTH THE DIVINE LIGHT
AS THE LAMPSTAND

We need to overcome the leaving of the first love, to maintain the eating of Christ as the tree of life, and to shine forth the divine light as the lampstand (Rev. 2:5b). Love is related to life, and life is related to light. Love, life, and light are a trinity. If you make Christ the first in everything, you have love. If you have this love, you have life, and you will enjoy the Lord. If you have life, this life becomes light to you. The light of the lampstand, the church, shines forth corporately versus individualistically in the dark night of the church age.

TO KEEP THE TESTIMONY OF JESUS
AS THE SHINING OF THE LAMPSTAND
IN THEIR LOCALITY

If we are enjoying Christ as our love, life, and light, we will keep the testimony of Jesus as the shining of the lampstand in our locality (Rev. 12:17b). We will testify of Christ's person as God and as man and of Christ's human living, crucifixion, resurrection, ascension, descension, and second appearing. The shining of the light is a testimony. In every aspect of our daily life, we should be shining forth Christ. This shining is the shining of the lampstand.

We need to remember these four words that begin with the letter "l"—love, life, light, and lampstand. These four "l" words start with love. We must give the Lord Jesus the preeminence in every way and in everything to recover the first love. Then we will enjoy Him as the tree of life, and this life right away becomes the light of life (John 8:12). Then we will be shining in our daily life and corporately as the lampstand. Otherwise, the lampstand will be removed from us individually and from the church corporately. The Lord warned the church in Ephesus to repent and recover the first love for the enjoyment of Him. Otherwise, the lampstand would be removed from them. We need love, life, light, and the lampstand. Then we will be rewarded by the Lord with what we are and live in Him.

In the Bible, the principle is that our reward is always what we are. What we are will become our reward. If we love others, our loving others will be a reward to us. If we honor our parents, our honor to them will be a reward to us. If we do not live Christ and behave in Christ in the church life, there will be nothing as a reward to us in the church life. Instead, because we do not live Christ, we may feel bitter toward the elders and toward all the saints. If we live Christ and behave in Christ, this living, this behaving, will become our reward. Then we will be happy in the church life. If today we take Christ as the first in everything, we will have love, we will enjoy Him as life, we will shine forth with Him as light, and we will become the shining lampstand as the testimony of Jesus. This eventually will become our reward not only in this age but even more in the coming age. In the thousand-year kingdom we will enjoy Christ as our reward in the Paradise of God.

CHAPTER THREE

TO OVERCOME PERSECUTION, WORLDLINESS, AND SPIRITUAL DEATH

Scripture Reading: Rev. 2:8-13, 17b; 3:1-5

OUTLINE

I. To overcome persecution, comprising tribulation, poverty, trial, imprisonment, and the slander of the deformed religion of Satan—Rev. 2:9-10a:
   A. By being faithful unto death, not loving the soul-life—2:10b; 12:11b.
   B. The reward:
      1. To receive the crown of life—2:10c.
      2. Not to be hurt by the second death—2:11.
II. To overcome worldliness:
   A. In a church that is affiliated with the world, where Satan administrates on his throne and dwells for his possession—2:13.
   B. To overcome such worldliness is to hold fast the name of the Lord and not deny the faith concerning the Lord—2:13.
   C. The reward—2:17b:
      1. To be given to eat of the hidden manna (Christ for nourishment).
      2. To be given a white stone (for the building in the Body of Christ), upon which a new name is written, which no one knows except he who receives it.
III. To overcome spiritual death:
   A. In a church having a name that it is living and

yet being dead, with nothing completed before God—3:1-2.
B. To overcome spiritual death is to be watchful and establish the things of life, which are about to die, and not to be defiled with the stain of spiritual death—3:2, 4.
C. The reward:
1. Not to miss the Lord in His coming secretly as a thief—3:3b.
2. To be clothed in white (signifying being justified and approved by the Lord in the purity of life) and walk with the Lord—3:4-5a.
3. To have his name never erased out of the book of life but confessed by the Lord before His Father and His Father's angels—3:5b.

In the previous chapter, we saw that we need to be those who overcome the loss of the first love by giving Christ the first place, the preeminence, in everything. The loss of the first love is seen with the church in Ephesus. There are four main points in the Lord's epistle to the church in Ephesus—love, life, light, and the lampstand (Rev. 2:4-5, 7). Love, life, and light are actually God Himself. God is love (1 John 4:8, 16), God is life (John 5:26; 14:6a), and God is light (1 John 1:5).

Actually, the Divine Trinity is love, life, and light. The Father is love, the Son is life, and the Spirit is light. The Father is the source as love, the Son is the course as life, and the Spirit is the flow as light. The Gospel of John says clearly, "In Him was life, and the life was the light of men" (1:4). Then the Lord said in John 8:12 that He was the light of the world and that whoever followed Him would have the light of life. The Bible eventually reveals that the Father is the Son (Isa. 9:6), and the Son is the Spirit (2 Cor. 3:17). This means that love is life, and life is light. Love is the source, life is the course, and light is the shining out to reach us. These are three aspects of one person. The Father, the Son, and the Spirit are one, so love, life, and light are one. We enjoy the Son as the divine life, the eternal life, the uncreated life, through the Spirit as light, and we touch the Father as love by the Son as life. The Triune God is love as the source, life as the course, and light as the flow to reach us. Every day and even every moment we are under the shining of the light, which means that we are under the reaching of the Triune God for our enjoyment. When we overcome to return to Christ as our first love, we will enjoy Him as life, and will shine forth the divine light as the lampstand to keep the testimony of Jesus (Rev. 1:9; 12:17) in our locality.

We have some hints about the overcomers in Paul's writings, but only the apostle John in the book of Revelation speaks directly concerning the overcomers. We have seen that the book of Revelation covers two main things—the overcomers and the New Jerusalem. The overcomers issue in the New Jerusalem, and the New Jerusalem is the consummation of the overcomers. The overcomers are precious stones, precious material, built together into a house, and this house is the consummation of all of the precious stones, the precious material. The house is the consummation, the building up, of all the precious stones.

In the beginning of Revelation, the Lord is calling for this precious material, for the overcomers. The Lord's calling in Revelation is not for being saved but for becoming an overcomer, a precious stone for God's building. The overcomers are the believers of Christ transformed into precious stones for the building of God. According to Revelation 2:17 every transformed believer as a white stone will bear a new name. This new name is the transformed name of a transformed person. In Revelation 2 and 3, the overcomers are not yet because the Lord is calling for them. Through the centuries, in the period of time from Revelation 4—20, the Lord has gained and is gaining a number of overcomers.

In this age the overcoming believers must pay the price to be built up together into one. There should be oneness among the saints and among all the co-workers. The Scriptures show that eventually there was no building between Paul and Barnabas. They were together for awhile, but after the conference in Jerusalem in Acts 15, there was a great split between Barnabas and Paul (vv. 35-39). Apollos was another problem. Paul told the Corinthians that he had urged Apollos to come to them many times. No doubt, the Corinthians were in desperate need, so he wanted Apollos to visit them, but Paul said, "It was not at all his desire to come now, but he will come when he has opportunity" (1 Cor. 16:12). By this we can see that Apollos was not one with Paul. But Paul and Timothy and Titus were one. When Paul told Timothy or Titus to go, they went. When he asked them to remain, they remained. But between Paul and Apollos there was not such a pleasant oneness; there was a big shortage of being built up.

Thus, we can see that between Paul and Barnabas, there was the lack of building, and between Paul and Apollos there was also the lack of building. If we consider the situation among Christians today, we will see that no one is built up with others. Everyone is independent. The big speakers in

Christianity build up something for themselves, but who is built up with others? To receive Christ as life for our regeneration is the initiation of our Christian life. To grow in this life is the second step. Then by this growth, we are transformed. After being transformed, we have to be built up together. This building is the consummation.

In this chapter we want to cover the three crucial points concerning the overcomers in the epistles to the church in Smyrna, the church in Pergamos, and the church in Sardis. The epistle to the church in Ephesus covers the overcoming of the loss of the first love. In the previous chapter, we saw the spiritual interpretation of the loss of the first love. To have the Lord as our first love actually means that we take our Lord as the first. We have to give Him the preeminence in everything. In everything He is the first. If we are not making Him the first in everything, we do not have the first love.

To have the first love is to give the preeminence, the first place, to the Lord Jesus in everything, even in all of the small things. When the brothers buy a tie, they need to give Christ the preeminence. When the sisters go shopping, they need to give Christ the first place. When the Saturday edition of the newspaper comes out, some sisters like to read it to find all of the sales in the department stores. To have this practice means that they do not give the Lord the preeminence. They do not let the Lord have the first place in their shopping. If we need something, we should go to the store to get that thing and nothing else. The sisters need to overcome the temptation of the department stores.

With the church in Ephesus, the Lord reveals that if we are going to overcome all the situations and be a real overcomer, we have to give the Lord the preeminence in everything. Then we will be ones who enjoy the Lord as the tree of life. First, we have love, and then we have life. Then corporately we will be the lampstand shining forth the divine light. Thus, we will have the four "l's"—love, life, light, and the lampstand. This is the revelation in the first epistle, which is to the church in Ephesus.

I. TO OVERCOME PERSECUTION, COMPRISING TRIBULATION, POVERTY, TRIAL, IMPRISONMENT, AND THE SLANDER OF THE DEFORMED RELIGION OF SATAN

The second epistle is written to Smyrna. This epistle reveals that we need to overcome persecution, comprising tribulation, poverty, trial, imprisonment, and the slander of the deformed religion of Satan (Rev. 2:9-10a). Smyrna basically shows us only one thing—persecution. Do we love the Lord? Do we give Him the preeminence in everything? If we do, we must be prepared for persecution.

Persecution will come to us from many directions. Persecution may come to a brother from his wife. When he did not love the Lord as the first item in everything, he had no problem with his wife. But when he began to love the Lord by giving Him the preeminence in everything, his wife noticed that he was different. Now her husband was giving the preeminence to someone else besides her.

In my home town of Chefoo, we had a brother who was working in the Chinese customs making good money. He was very worldly, and his wife was very happy to go along with him in their pursuit of worldly amusements. One day, however, he began to love the Lord, giving the Lord the preeminence. He gave the Lord the first place in everything. That was a big change with him. As a result, the wife became very unhappy because her husband no longer desired the things of the world.

Because this brother had such a positive change toward the Lord, he wanted to invite some brothers to his home for fellowship. He told his wife that one evening he would invite a few brothers to their house for dinner. I was one among these brothers. We all went happily to this brother's home for fellowship. When we sat down to eat, his wife served us with cold leftovers. The brother felt so bad about this that he was moved to tears. Instead of being affected by the situation, however, we all partook of the food set before us in a joyful way in support of our brother. This brother suffered much persecution from his wife because of his decision to make the Lord first in everything.

Some parents persecute their children because of their children's love for the Lord, and some children persecute their parents because of their parents' love for the Lord. The mother-in-law may persecute her daughter-in-law for loving the Lord. This is why the Lord said that a man who puts Him first will have enemies from his own household (Matt. 10:36). The persecution revealed in the epistle to the church in Smyrna comprises tribulation, poverty, trial, imprisonment, and the slander of the deformed religion of Satan. The deformed religion of Satan was the synagogue of Satan (Rev. 2:9). At the Lord's time and at the early apostles' time, the synagogues of the Jews had become in the eyes of God the synagogue of Satan.

According to history the saints during the time of Smyrna had tribulation for ten days (v. 10). As a sign, the ten days here indicate prophetically the ten periods of persecution that the church suffered under the Roman emperors, beginning with Caesar Nero in the second half of the first century and ending with Constantine the Great in the first part of the fourth century. Roman history tells us that the Roman Empire had ten periods of time to persecute the Christians.

We may feel that unlike the saints in Smyrna we have a good government today, but persecution can come to us from many other directions. Thus, as the loving seekers of Jesus, we must be prepared to suffer. The martyrs for Christ can be martyrs physically. Paul suffered such a martyrdom (2 Tim. 4:6). Many of us, however, may not suffer a physical martyrdom, but a psychological martyrdom or a spiritual martyrdom. The aforementioned brother who was mistreated by his wife was surely a martyr under her persecution. He used to come to us for fellowship, and we tried our best to support him and comfort him. In a very positive sense, he was a martyr for the Lord's interest. He would not change in his feeling for the Lord, and he has never changed.

Even among the elders in the church, there may be the experience of martyrdom. One brother among the elders might be very strong and controlling. He may be a good brother who loves the Lord and the church, but he controls the other elders. The other elders may feel that they cannot function under such a brother, and they may want to resign. Someone may ask them, "Don't you love the Lord? Don't you love the church? Don't you have a loving care for all the saints?" They would say that they do, but they find it unbearable to serve under such a strong brother. But if these brothers resign, this means that they resign from martyrdom. Thus, they are missing the opportunity to be martyred, an opportunity which may never return in their lifetime. How good it is for these elders to be martyred under a strong brother who is like a dictator!

In 1935 and 1936, I was assigned to the work in northern China. The elders in the church in Peking could not get along with one another. They frequently wanted me to come and help them. I spent two or three days to fellowship with them, and they felt that their problems were solved, but a week later they called me again to come and help them because they still could not get along. These elders had the opportunity to be overcoming martyrs in the church life.

When the apostle Paul asked the Lord three times to remove the thorn from him, the Lord's response was, "My grace is sufficient for you" (2 Cor. 12:9). The Lord allowed the thorn to remain with Paul so that Paul would be able to enjoy the Lord as his all-sufficient grace. Sufferings, trials, and persecution are often ordained by the Lord for us that we may experience Him as grace. Hence, in spite of Paul's entreaty, the Lord would not remove the thorn from him.

We do not need to travel all over the earth to experience suffering and persecution. There is persecution for us to experience in our local church. There is a narrow door at the front of the church life, but once we make the choice to enter into the church life, there are no "back doors" and no "fire escapes." In a sense, all of the saints in the church life become our persecutors. When we initially came into the church life, everyone was pleasant to us. That was our church life honeymoon, but the honeymoon does not last long. After we have stayed in the church life for a number of years, we realize that the Lord uses nearly all of the saints to deal with us.

Some saints told me that they could not bear to stay in

their locality and that they wanted me to help them choose a better place. I always say that the best place is the present place. No place is better than the present place. Many saints eventually were convinced by me. They realized that they should not move to another locality according to their personal preference. If they move to another locality according to their choice, the place to which they move will eventually be worse to them than the place from which they came. In the church life, we cannot avoid "persecution."

We need to overcome all kinds of persecution by being faithful unto death, not loving our soul-life (Rev. 2:10b; 12:11b). Then we will be rewarded with the crown of life (2:10c), and we will not be hurt by the second death (2:11).

II. TO OVERCOME WORLDLINESS

Now we come to the church in Pergamos (Rev. 2:12). History tells us that the church during the age of Pergamos became altogether worldly. The Greek word for Pergamos means marriage (implying union). This indicates that the church in Pergamos became one with the world as in the union of marriage. The church in Pergamos married herself to the world. This marriage took place when Constantine welcomed Christianity as the state religion in the first part of the fourth century. The Lord charged the saints to overcome in such a worldly situation. If they would overcome, He would give them to eat of the hidden manna (Rev. 2:17).

When the people of Israel were wandering in the wilderness, God fed them for forty years every morning with manna in a public way. But Moses was also told to take some manna, put it into a golden pot, and place this golden pot in the ark within the Holy of Holies for a memorial before God (Exo. 16:32-34). In Revelation the Lord promised the faithful saints in Pergamos that if they would remain faithful, He would give them to eat of the hidden manna, which signifies that Christ as the special portion allotted to the saints becomes a hidden portion to the faithful ones.

When we are being persecuted either by our parents, by our relatives, by the elders, by the co-workers, or by the dear saints, and we would not resist or resign but would remain

with and in the Lord in this situation, the Lord Jesus will
be the hidden manna to us. A particular portion of Christ, a
special portion, will be our hidden manna. This special portion
will become our support and our strength. How can we endure
suffering and live in a situation in which no one else can live?
We can endure because we daily enjoy the Lord Jesus as a
special portion, the hidden manna.

The Lord also promised the faithful ones at Pergamos that
He would give them a white stone on which a new name is
written (Rev. 2:17). If we do not follow the worldly church
but enjoy the Lord in the proper church life, we will be
transformed into stones for the building of God. There are
millions of Christians today, but it is difficult to see any one
of them built up together with others. We are not built up
with others because we all have our peculiar traits. This is why
there are many separations and divorces among husbands
and wives. The husband and wife cannot be built up together
because of their peculiar traits.

In like manner, we cannot be built up together in the
church life because of our peculiarities. We all have our particular, peculiar traits. This is why we need to be transformed.
It would be helpful for us to sing the following hymn (*Hymns,*
#750) on transformation with our heart and with our spirit.

> God's intention is to have us
>   All conformed to His dear Son;
> Thus a work of transformation
>   By the Spirit must be done.

> Lord, transform us to Thine image
>   In emotion, mind, and will;
> Saturate us with Thy Spirit,
>   All our being wholly fill.

> God hath us regenerated
>   In our spirit with His life;
> But He must transform us further—
>   In our soul by His own life.

> Spreading outward from our spirit
> Doth the Lord transform our soul,
> By the inward parts renewing,
> Till within His full control.
>
> By the power of His Spirit
> In His pattern He transforms;
> From His glory to His glory
> To His image He conforms.
>
> He transforms, all sanctifying,
> Till like Him we are matured;
> He transforms, our soul possessing,
> Till His stature is secured.

We need such transformation. Then we will no longer be natural, and we will be able to be built up together. God desires a house, not individual pieces of material. God wants all the individual material to be built together to be His house, to be His Body. Therefore, today our urgent need is to be transformed.

The Lord promised the overcomers in Pergamos two things: first, the hidden manna for their support and supply and second, a white stone, indicating that they will be the material for God's building. In our natural being we are not stones but clay. Because we received the divine life with its divine nature through regeneration, we can be transformed into stones, even precious stones (1 Cor. 3:12), by enjoying Christ as our life supply (2 Cor. 3:18).

When Simon came to the Lord, the Lord immediately changed his name to Peter, which means *a stone* (John 1:42). In the four Gospels, Peter was a difficult case among all the disciples. He was very peculiar, but the Lord dealt with him to get him transformed. In his old age he said in his first Epistle that we are called to be living stones to be built up into a corporate priesthood, that is, a corporate building as God's spiritual house (1 Pet. 2:5). This is what God desires.

Today the Lord has put us in certain circumstances so that we can learn the lessons of transformation. In the church life, we should not have any choice nor should we try to initiate any change. We should remain where we are to suffer joyfully so that we can be transformed. Then we will no longer be men of clay but stones, even white stones. Being white indicates that we are justified by the Lord and approved by Him, that He is happy with us. When we are transformed, we can be properly and adequately built up with others. This is what the epistle to the church in Pergamos shows us.

The Lord's word to Pergamos indicates that we need to overcome worldliness in a church that is married to the world, where Satan administrates on his throne and dwells for his possession (Rev. 2:13). To overcome such worldliness is to hold fast the name of the Lord and not deny the faith concerning the Lord (v. 13). If we are faithful to overcome, the Lord will give us to eat of the hidden manna (Christ for our particular nourishment), and He will give us a white stone (for the building in the Body of Christ), upon which a new name is written (according to our new experiences of the particular Christ), which no one knows except he who receives it (v. 17). God's work of building the church depends on our transformation, and our transformation issues from the enjoyment of Christ as the hidden manna, our life supply.

III. TO OVERCOME SPIRITUAL DEATH

Now we come to the church in Sardis. The church in Sardis signifies today's Protestant churches. The Lord said that those in Sardis had a name that they were living, but in actuality they were not living; they were dead and dying (Rev. 3:1-2). This indicates that on the one hand, they had died, but on the other hand, their death had not been completed. This is the situation in today's Protestant churches.

About two years ago, a number of leading ones in the denominations in the United States considered a proposal to evangelize the entire world. However, they concluded that they did not have the manpower, the personnel, to do it. According to recent statistics, there are approximately sixty-five million Protestant believers in the United States, which is more than one-fourth of the entire population. Even though the Protestant churches have sixty-five million Christians, they said that they did not have enough manpower. This is

because in today's Christianity there is no developing of
the saints' gifts in life, but there is an annulling, a killing
of death, of the functioning of the members of Christ's Body.
In a big denomination, only the pastor and his few assis-
tants and helpers are active. All the rest of the members
are considered as laymen. They have been busy with their
occupations all week, so on the weekend they like to come
to the Lord's Day morning service to rest. All of them are
accustomed to coming on the Lord's Day to hear a knowledge-
able, eloquent, and attractive speaker. They think that this
is reasonable. Such a practice, however, kills the spiritual
functions of all the attendants. This is why the Lord has led
us in these recent years to promote all the saints prophesying
(1 Cor. 14:3), speaking for the Lord.

According to God's ordination, the practice of the church
life is not with one man speaking and the rest listening. The
church practice is what Paul teaches in 1 Corinthians 14. In
this chapter he says that we can all prophesy one by one
(v. 31). We must pray that the Lord will develop our capacity,
our ability, to speak for Him. All of us should be living members of Christ seeking to speak for the Lord and to speak forth
the Lord in the church meetings for the building up of the
church as the Body of Christ (v. 4b) in a living way. We should
by no means be dead and dying. We may not be able to give a
long message, but at least we can speak for the Lord for three
minutes. We should seek to excel for the building up of the
church (v. 12).

Today's practice of one man speaking and the rest listening makes the church not only dormant but also dead and
dying. Only a minority are working in today's Christianity;
the rest are dead and dying. We need to practice the church
meetings according to what is revealed in 1 Corinthians 14.
Verse 1 says, "Pursue love, and desire earnestly spiritual
gifts, but especially that you may prophesy." Some opposers
have said 1 Corinthians 14 was not written to all the saints
but to a group of prophets. But verse 1 shows us that this
chapter was written to all the saints. We all have to pursue
love; we all have to desire earnestly spiritual gifts; and we all
have to especially desire to prophesy.

If we do not speak for the Lord, this is a loss to ourselves, to the church, and to the Lord's interest on this earth. The more we speak, the more we will have to speak, and the more we will receive for us to release. When we speak in a meeting, that meeting will be wonderful to us. The meeting was good to us because we spoke. But if we do not speak in the meeting, that meeting will be a poor meeting to us. The meeting was poor to us because we did not speak. When we prophesy we edify ourselves, we perfect others, and we build up the Body of Christ. If one hundred saints are meeting together on the Lord's Day, and thirty exercise their spirits to speak for the Lord, this meeting will be very refreshing and living. This kind of prophesying will make the church living in every way through every member.

In the past seven and a half years, we have been stressing that we need to take the God-ordained way. We need to rise up to practice the New Testament priesthood of the gospel, preaching the gospel by visiting people regularly to get people saved. Then all the time we will have new ones baptized into the church life. If we practice the priesthood of the gospel, the entire church will be active and living.

Then we all have to bear the burden to feed the young ones, to nourish the new babes in Christ. If we labor in the Lord according to His ordained way, we will not have the time to gossip. We should not be the "information desk" of the church life. Instead, we should speak for the Lord by speaking the gospel to sinners, by speaking the nourishing word to the young ones, by speaking to perfect the saints, and by speaking to build up the Body of Christ.

We surely do not want to be in the condition of the church in Sardis. We want to be living and active in gospel preaching, in nourishing the new ones, in perfecting the saints, and in prophesying to build up the Body of Christ. We need the new ones in the church life. We need to nourish the new ones until they become remaining fruit in the church life. Then we should speak in the meetings, to set up a pattern for all the young ones to follow. Children learn how to speak from their parents. The church must be like this. Then from generation to generation all the young ones will grow and be perfected to do the work of the apostles, prophets, evangelists, and shepherds and teachers (Eph. 4:11-12). This will make the church very living, active, functioning, and working according to the Lord's desire.

Thus, we have seen that we need to overcome persecution, to overcome worldliness by being transformed, and to overcome spiritual death by being living. We should be ready to suffer any kind of persecution. We also are destined to grow that we might be transformed to be built up. Furthermore, we have to be living. When we sing, we should sing livingly. When we pray, we should pray livingly. When we preach the gospel, we should preach livingly. Everything we do in the church life should be living.

I hope to see such a scene in the church life. When we come to the meetings of the church, we should not wait for the elders to begin the meeting. Anyone can open up the meeting. We can begin the meeting by singing a hymn or by praying. This proves that the church is living. If we are waiting for the leading ones to begin the meeting, this shows that the church is dormant, dead, and dying. Actually, the meeting should begin from our homes. When we are eating dinner, we can sing a hymn together, pray, and fellowship with one another. Then as we are driving to the meeting, we should continue to exercise our spirit to sing to the Lord, pray to Him, and praise Him. When we come to the church meetings in this way, this is a strong sign that the church is living. We are not dead, but we are in resurrection, speaking for the Lord in a living way to build up His organic Body.

CHAPTER FOUR

TO OVERCOME THE
THREE DEFORMED RELIGIONS

Scripture Reading: Rev. 2:9b; Exo. 20:8-11; Gen. 17:10-14; Lev. 11; Luke 24:44; 2 Cor. 3:6; Gal. 1:6-16; Phil. 3:2-3; 2 Tim. 1:14; Matt. 13:33; Rev. 2:20, 24; 17:1, 5-6, 16; 14:8; 2 Tim. 4:7c; Rev. 2:26, 6, 14-15; Col. 1:18; 1 Cor. 14:23a, 24, 26, 31, 3-5; Phil. 3:10; 1:19b

OUTLINE

I. Judaism:
   A. A religion set up, though not fully, according to the decree of the law of God, but deformed by man and becoming a satanic religion—"a synagogue of Satan"—Rev. 2:9b:
      1. Mis-positioning the law given by God as a side line to Christ as the main line in His economy.
      2. Misapplying the dispensational Sabbath-keeping—Exo. 20:8-11.
      3. Misinterpreting the physical circumcision—Gen. 17:10-14.
      4. Overstretching the holy diet—Lev. 11.
   B. Disregarding Christ as the embodiment of the Triune God ordained by God to be the centrality and universality of His economy, as:
      1. Typified by the tabernacle, the priesthood, and the offerings in the five books of the Law.
      2. Prophesied in the Law of Moses, the Prophets, and the Psalms—Luke 24:44.
   C. Becoming formal in letter, deadening in quenching the Spirit, killing in man's communication with

God in life, and contending with the gospel of Christ in God's New Testament economy—2 Cor. 3:6; Gal. 1:6-16; Phil. 3:2-3.

D. To overcome such a satanic religion by holding to the teaching of the apostles (the New Testament) through the all-inclusive life-giving Spirit—2 Tim. 1:14.

II. Catholicism:

A. A woman having leavened the "three measures of meal" (the entire teaching concerning the element of Christ in His person and in His work)—Matt. 13:33.

B. The woman Jezebel, who calls herself a prophetess, teaching and leading the people of God, even with "the deep things of Satan"—Rev. 2:20, 24:

  1. To propagate fornication.

  2. To promote idolatry.

C. Built up as a religious hierarchy.

D. "The great harlot," "Mystery, Babylon the Great, the mother of the harlots and the abominations of the earth," adopting many heathen practices—Rev. 17:1, 5.

E. Martyring the saints and the witnesses of Jesus—Rev. 17:6.

F. To be hated, made desolate, and burned by Antichrist and his ten kings at the beginning of the great tribulation—Rev. 17:16; 14:8.

G. To overcome such a heretical religion by keeping the faith in Christ's divine and human person and all His works in His incarnation, crucifixion, resurrection, ascension, descension, and second appearing—2 Tim. 4:7c; Rev. 2:26.

III. Protestantism:

A. Practicing the works of the Nicolaitans (the works of the clergy in the religious hierarchy)—Rev. 2:6.

B. Holding the teaching of Balaam, who put a stumbling block before the people of God, to accept idolatry and commit fornication—Rev. 2:14.

C. Holding the teaching of the Nicolaitans to build up hierarchy and practice the system of clergy—Rev. 2:15.

D. Disregarding Christ's headship in His Body—Col. 1:18.

E. Annulling the functions of the members in the Body of Christ.

F. Keeping most of the church meetings for the service of the clergy, while having nearly no meeting for the manifestation of the gifts of all the members of the Body for the organic building up of the Body of Christ in the unsearchable riches of Christ—cf. 1 Cor. 14:23a, 24, 26, 31, 3-5.

G. To overcome such a dead and dying religion by the pneumatic Christ in His resurrection and the bountiful supply of the all-inclusive Spirit—Phil. 3:10; 1:19b.

Thus far, we have seen that we need to overcome the leaving of the first love, to overcome persecution, to overcome worldliness, and to overcome spiritual death. In this chapter we want to see that we need to overcome the three deformed religions—Judaism, Catholicism, and Protestantism.

We Christians have one Triune God—the Father, the Son, and the Spirit. We have one Bible, one divine revelation. We are also one church, one Body. We are the Body, the church, based upon the divine revelation revealed in the one Bible from the one Spirit, the one Son, and the one Father—the one Triune God. If there were no religion, how good this would be! We should be those who hate religion and who love the one Triune God, the one Father, one Son, and one Spirit; the one Bible, the one divine revelation; and the one church, the one Body.

In every religion there are satanic and devilish things, including falsehood, heresy, and idolatry. In the book of Revelation, the Roman Catholic Church is seen as a great harlot with many daughters (Rev. 17:1, 5). The Bible does not tell us how many daughters this great harlot has, but undoubtedly she has many. We have to expose this situation. Every religion must be exposed in our enlightened eyes that we may clearly see the Triune God—the Father, the Son, the Spirit; the Holy Bible, the divine revelation; and the church, the Body of Christ.

Today we have one Bible, yet many who claim to have one Bible are always contending about things in the Bible. One person has one interpretation, and another person has another. There have been many debates and conflicts throughout church history concerning the Triune God. These doctrinal debates and different interpretations of the Bible have given Satan the ground to deceive people and to seduce them to make religions.

Today there are four major religions: Judaism, Catholicism, Protestantism, and Mohammedanism (Islam), which may be considered as a false copy of Judaism. These four religions are very prevailing. We need to consider where we are today. We are not in Judaism, Catholicism, Protestantism, nor Mohammedanism. We are in the one Triune God—one Father, one Son, and one Spirit; in the one Bible, the one divine revelation; and in the one church, the one Body of Christ. In this chapter we want to fellowship about the three deformed religions revealed in the book of Revelation—Judaism, Catholicism, and Protestantism. Each of these three religions is not simple.

I. JUDAISM

Judaism is the religion of the Jews. The Jewish people have the oldest history. The first five books of the Bible, the Pentateuch, were written in approximately 1500 B.C. The Bible covers human history beginning from the creation of Adam about six thousand years ago. From Adam to Abraham was two thousand years, from Abraham to Christ was also two thousand years, and from Christ until today has been about two thousand years. Then there will be another period of one thousand years, the millennium. Thus, this holy Book covers the history of mankind in time for at least seven thousand years, the entire span of human history. It speaks of the first generation of mankind with Adam and of the second generation with Abel. Then it continues to reveal the generations of human history until today. All the basic factors of the Jewish religion are revealed in the Bible.

A. A Religion Set Up, Though Not Fully, according to the Decree of the Law of God, but Deformed by Man and Becoming a Satanic Religion—"a Synagogue of Satan"

Judaism is a religion which was set up, though not fully, according to the decree of the law of God. The law of God decreed by God through Moses is a good base, but this religion was deformed by man to become a satanic religion— "a synagogue of Satan." In Revelation 2:9b the Lord refers to "the slander from those who call themselves Jews and are not, but are a synagogue of Satan." The Judaizers called themselves Jews but they were not Jews. They were Jews in the flesh but not Jews in the spirit (Rom. 2:28-29). Merely being the seed of Abraham did not constitute them true Jews.

Those who are the children of the flesh are not the children of God (Rom. 9:7-8).

Revelation 2:9b reveals that Judaism is a satanic religion. This verse tells us that the synagogue of the Jews today is not of God but of Satan. This shows that the religious Jews worship God in name, but actually they are one with Satan, God's enemy.

1. Mis-positioning the Law
Given by God as a Side Line to
Christ as the Main Line in His Economy

The Jewish religion has mis-positioned the law given by God as a side line to Christ as the main line in His economy. In his Epistle to the Galatians, Paul used two women in the Old Testament in Genesis to signify two things (4:22-31). These two women are Sarah, Abraham's wife, and Hagar, Abraham's concubine. Sarah signifies God's grace and Hagar signifies God's law. The position of the law is that of a concubine, and the position of God's grace is that of a proper wife. The law was given by God and is of God, but God put the law into the position of a concubine. The Jewish people made the mistake of positioning the law as a wife. This means that they mis-positioned the law.

God gave the law as a side line to Christ, who is the main line in God's economy. In God's economy there are two lines; one is the main line, and the other is the side line. The main line is Christ and the side line is the law. The Bible teaches mainly Christ. Christ is the main subject of the Bible. Christ stands as the main line and even the main lane of the Bible. When we drive a car, we do not want to drive in the side lane but in the main lane. We are driving in Christ, taking Christ as our main lane and main line. The Jews, however, are on the side line, remaining with the law as a concubine.

One among the Jews, Saul of Tarsus, later became an apostle. He tried his best to correct the Jews because they were not in the main line. Judaism is satanic because it does not stay in God's ordained line. According to the Bible, God gave the law to help the Jews realize that they could not keep the law. To try to keep the law is foolish. Instead, we should remain with Christ. We should not get away from Christ. He is our main line. Paul took Christ in such a way, but the Jews would not take Paul's advice.

According to Paul's word in Romans 7, the law is the instrument through which sin deceives and kills men (v. 11). The power of sin is the law (1 Cor. 15:56). This fact should warn us not to turn to the law to try to keep it, for in so doing we give sin the opportunity to deceive and kill us. Those in Judaism have all been killed by the law. There are five million members of Judaism in the United States today, and all of them have been distracted from Christ. They are on the side line of the law committing "suicide." Hagar, typifying the law, and her son were cast out (Gal. 4:30-31). Thus those under the slavery of the law are driven out of God's grace.

Hagar brought forth a son named Ishmael. There are many Ishmaelites today fighting against Israel. The issue of Hagar is one who fights against God's people. Ishmael persecuted Isaac (Gen. 21:9). The Judaizers, the descendants of Abraham according to the flesh, also persecuted the believers, the descendants of Abraham according to the Spirit, as Ishmael persecuted Isaac (Gal. 4:29).

2. Misapplying the Dispensational Sabbath-keeping

Those in Judaism also have misapplied the dispensational Sabbath-keeping (Exo. 20:8-11). In history God set up a day called the Sabbath. God created the heavens and earth and millions of things within six days. After these six days, God declared the seventh day as a day of rest. The Sabbath was God's rest. Then God charged His people to keep that day as a memorial of God's creation. Man was charged to keep the Sabbath to remember God's creation, that is, to remember that Jehovah, *Elohim,* is the Creator of the universe and of man.

We need to realize, however, that God's ordination concerning the keeping of the Sabbath was a dispensational ordination. In the Bible God has different ways to deal with people in different ages. In the early age of God's dealing with man, there was an ordination for man to keep the Sabbath. That ordination was for that age. It was not an

eternal ordination but a dispensational ordination. When
that dispensation, or period of time, was over, the keeping
of the Sabbath was over.

The Jews, however, did not realize this, so they misapplied
the dispensational Sabbath-keeping. Before Jesus came,
Moses charged Israel to keep the Sabbath. That was according to God's charge. When Jesus came, however, He was
the Sabbath as the rest for God's people (Matt. 11:28-30). The
Sabbath was a type, a shadow, of Christ. When the person
comes, the shadow is over. We should not keep the shadow
when we have the person. When the person is here with us we
do not disregard him to pay attention to his photo. That
would be foolish. Thus, when Jesus came, the outward ritual
of keeping the Sabbath was over.

The Jews fought against Jesus mainly due to the keeping
of the Sabbath day. The observance of the Sabbath was abol-
ished by the Lord Jesus in His ministry (Matt. 12:1-12). That
offended the Jews to the uttermost. They wanted to destroy
Him because of this (v. 14; John 5:16). Thus, they misapplied
the keeping of the Sabbath.

3. Misinterpreting the Physical Circumcision

The Jews also misinterpret the ordinance of physical
circumcision (Gen. 17:10-14). In order to keep His chosen
people a particular people, different from the Gentiles, God
ordained that they practice circumcision. Physically speaking, circumcision is the cutting off of a piece of flesh. This
cutting off, in a physical sense, does not mean anything to our
inward being subjectively.

Actually, circumcision signifies that the chosen people of
God should cut off the flesh. This is the real significance
of circumcision, but the Jews misinterpreted it, making the
physical act of circumcision very important. Many Jewish
believers insisted that unless people were circumcised according to the custom of Moses, they could not be saved (Acts 15:1).
This was an annulling of the faith in God's New Testament
economy and a real heresy, causing a big confrontation in
Acts 15. Circumcision was a shadow of the crucifixion of
Christ in its putting off of the flesh, as signified in baptism

(Col. 2:11-12). The practice of circumcision was counted as nothing in the revelation received by Paul in his ministry (Gal. 5:6; 6:15).

4. Overstretching the Holy Diet

The adherents of Judaism also overstretched the holy diet. In Leviticus 11 God charged His chosen people, Israel, to take care of their eating in a particular way, not following the Gentiles. All the nations, the Gentiles, eat many unclean, defiling things. God is wise. The diet revealed in Leviticus is a very healthy diet, but we need to see that these dietary ordinances were also dispensational.

The holy dietary regulations were annulled by the Spirit in Peter's ministry (Acts 10:9-20). God wanted to use Peter to preach the gospel to the Gentiles, but the Jews would not contact the Gentiles. To the Jews the Gentiles were as unclean animals. One day Peter saw a heavenly vision of a great sheet descending from heaven, full of unclean animals. A heavenly voice said, "Rise up, Peter; slay and eat!" (v. 13). Peter refused to do so because he had never eaten anything common and unclean. This happened three times, and then the great sheet was taken up into heaven. The heavenly vision which Peter received annulled the dietary regulations in Leviticus 11.

Actually, the holy diet symbolizes persons who are clean and persons who are unclean, those whom God's holy people should contact and those they should not contact (Acts 10:11-16, 34-35). God revealed to Peter that these unclean animals in his vision were actually people and that he should not call any man whom God has cleansed by the redeeming blood of Christ common or unclean (vv. 15, 28). Peter was taught by the Lord in such a way, but when he was in Antioch, he shrank back and separated himself from the Gentiles out of fear of those of the circumcision. Peter became a hypocrite (Gal. 2:11-14). All of this shows that the Jewish religion had overstretched the significance of the holy diet.

Thus, the law with the practice of circumcision, the Sabbath, and the holy diet constituted Judaism, which was deformed by man to become a religion of Satan. The law was given not for God's chosen people to keep, but for God's people to be tested, to be exposed, so that they could see that they are sinful and wicked. We have no capacity to keep the law. Instead, we should put our trust absolutely and fully in Christ. In our life-study of the Psalms we pointed out that the intention of the Psalms is not to charge us to keep the law but to turn us away from the law to Christ. Paul said clearly in Galatians 2 that if righteousness is through the law, Christ has died for nothing (v. 21). Thus, we can see that the Jewish religion has become satanic, "a synagogue of Satan."

B. Disregarding Christ as the Embodiment of the Triune God, Ordained by God to Be the Centrality and Universality of His Economy

The Jewish religion missed Christ and also disregarded Christ. In the Pentateuch, the first five books of the Bible, there are many prophecies and types concerning Christ. The Jews missed all these prophecies and types because they regarded only the law and disregarded Christ as the embodiment of the Triune God (Col. 2:9). Outside of Christ and without Him, we do not have the Triune God. The Jews think that they are worshipping God, *Elohim,* Jehovah, but they do not realize that Jehovah *Elohim* is embodied in Christ. The entire Triune God is in Christ, so outside of Christ we cannot find God. Christ is God's dwelling place. Christ is God's address. Christ is God's home. If you want God, yet do not want Christ, you cannot have God.

The Jews also were the ones who desired to crucify Christ. They shouted again and again, "Crucify Him!" and their voice won (Mark 15:13-14). They did not realize that this Christ as the embodiment of God was ordained by God to be the centrality and universality of His economy. If you disregard Him, you disregard everything.

Christ was typified by the tabernacle, the priesthood, and the offerings in the five books of the Law. God put something very substantial in the Torah. These substantial things were the tabernacle and the corporate priesthood daily serving God in the tabernacle with all the offerings. The Jews took these things formally. They never understood what these things signified. They did not realize that the tabernacle is a type of Christ (John 1:14) to be God's dwelling place for God's people to contact God, to enter into God, and to enjoy God. When the Jewish people sinned, they knew that the law ordered them to offer a trespass offering, but they did not realize that this offering was a type of Christ. They had the substantial types, but they did not understand their significance, so they spontaneously disregarded Christ.

The Lord's word in Luke 24:44 shows that He was prophesied in the Law of Moses, the Prophets, and the Psalms. In Genesis 3:15 God promised that the seed of the woman would come to bruise the head of the serpent. That was a clear prophecy about Christ. Then God prophesied to Abraham that all the nations would be blessed through his seed, and that seed is Christ (Gen. 22:18; Gal. 3:16). Isaiah says clearly that a virgin shall bring forth a child whose name is called Immanuel (Isa. 7:14). That child is God with man. This was a clear prophecy concerning Christ, but the Jews disregarded it. The Jews had the Old Testament, but they did not care for the prophecies concerning Christ.

C. Becoming Formal in Letter, Deadening in Quenching the Spirit, Killing in Man's Communication with God in Life, and Contending with the Gospel of Christ in God's New Testament Economy

Judaism became formal in letter and deadening in quenching the Spirit. The Jewish religion kills man's communication with God in life. Judaism also contended with the gospel of Christ in God's New Testament economy (2 Cor. 3:6; Gal. 1:6-16; Phil. 3:2-3). Under the maneuvering hand of Satan, those in Judaism opposed the Lord Jesus (Matt. 12:9-14; Luke 4:28-29; John 9:22). They also opposed the apostle Paul (Acts 13:45-46, 50; 14:1-2, 19; 17:1, 5-6). Acts 21 tells us that the Jews from Asia saw him in the temple in Jerusalem and seized him. As they were seeking to kill him, the Roman commander stopped them and took Paul into custody (vv. 27-33). Later, more than forty of the Jews formed a plot and put themselves under a curse, saying that they would neither eat nor drink until they had killed Paul (23:12-13). Eventually, he was transferred from Palestine to Rome to be judged directly by Caesar (25:9-12). This was the way that the Jews persecuted Paul, the Lord's servant. Thus, we can see that they disregarded Christ, annulled all the spiritual things, and contended against the gospel of Christ.

D. To Overcome Such a Satanic Religion by Holding to the Teaching of the Apostles

The way to overcome such a satanic religion is by holding to the teaching of the apostles (the New Testament) through the all-inclusive life-giving Spirit (2 Tim. 1:14). Our "Torah" today is the New Testament, the apostles' teaching. We have to hold to this teaching through the all-inclusive life-giving Spirit.

II. CATHOLICISM

A. A Woman Having Leavened the "Three Measures of Meal" (the Entire Teaching concerning the Element of Christ in His Person and in His Work)

In Matthew 13:33 Catholicism is typified by a woman who leavened the "three measures of meal," the entire teaching concerning the element of Christ in His person and in His work. The Catholic Church accepted the New Testament teaching, but they leavened it. Bread without leaven is hard to take. Leavened bread is soft and easy for people to eat. This is the reasoning of the Catholic Church. The Catholic people have so-called pictures of Jesus, and many of them believe that this is Jesus. If you ask the priests in the Catholic Church why they do this, they will say that Jesus is spiritual, mysterious, and hard for people to apprehend, so they need something physical like pictures or statues in order to apprehend Him. Our natural being likes to use certain things to make spiritual matters easier to assimilate. This is what the Bible calls leaven.

The so-called pictures of Jesus are of a handsome man, but Isaiah tells us that He had no comeliness or outward beauty (Isa. 53:2) and that His visage was marred more than that of any man (52:14). There is one Catholic cathedral in Manila with a statue of Jesus, and all the worshippers entering into the cathedral touch the feet of this statue. What a superstition this is! One brother who was brought up as a Catholic came into the Lord's recovery and began to see that Jesus lived in him, so he went back home to tell his relative. The relative responded that she also had Jesus, and she pointed to a picture of Jesus hanging on her wall. Such pictures and statues are idols.

In 1937 when I was traveling in North China, a case of demon possession was brought to my attention. A certain sister had become possessed. I checked with the saints concerning whether there were any idols in her home. Eventually, I learned that on the wall there was a picture of the so-called Jesus, and I told her to burn it. A number of Catholics kneel down, worship, and pray to this picture. When she burned that picture, the demon departed. Idols, including pictures and statues, are the means used by the demons to hide themselves. The so-called picture of Jesus is an idol. By this we can see that the Catholic Church is altogether superstitious.

At a Catholic cathedral in Manila, I saw many people purchasing candles and placing them before the images and idols on the walls. Some of these idols have inscriptions under them which say that if you pray a certain prayer every day for a period of time, you will reduce your dead relatives' time in purgatory. Purgatory in Roman Catholicism is a place where those who have died go to be purged of their sins through suffering.

Catholicism has taken in many pagan, idolatrous things. G. H. Pember pointed out in his book *The Great Prophecies* that Buddha is actually a saint in the Roman Catholic Calendar under the name of Saint Josaphat (see *Life-study of Revelation*, p. 585). This is why Revelation 2:24 says the Catholic Church has the deep things of Satan. The Roman Catholic Church has many satanic mysteries. Even the architecture of the Catholic cathedrals with their stained-glass

windows and high ceilings makes them very dark. In addition
to this, they are full of idols. In the Roman Catholic Church,
the worship of idols is taught. Idol worship is a kind of witch-
craft for contacting the demons.

The Catholic Church does not keep the pure truth but has
leavened the truths of the Bible with evil, heretical, and
pagan things. Once the meal is leavened there is no way to
purify it. Today the entire Catholic Church is a mixture of
truth with leaven. They admit that Christ is God, but they
call Mary the mother of God and say that she has no sin.
This shows again the heresy and superstition of the Roman
Catholic Church.

B. The Woman Jezebel
Calling Herself a Prophetess

Catholicism is portrayed as the woman Jezebel who calls
herself a prophetess, teaching and leading the people of God,
even with "the deep things of Satan" (Rev. 2:20, 24). Catholics
do not say, "The Bible says...." Instead, they say, "The church
says...." The church here is signified by Jezebel. The Catholic
Church today is the woman concerning whom the Lord prophesied in Matthew 13, and she is also the Jezebel spoken of in
Revelation 2. Jezebel was the pagan wife of Ahab, an evil king
(1 Kings 16:30-31), and she did many evil things (2 Kings
9:7). The Catholic Church in the eyes of God is like that evil
Jezebel, teaching heresies. This apostate church is a self-
appointed prophetess, one who presumes to be authorized by
God to speak for God.

The Catholic Church leads people into spiritual as well as
physical fornication (Rev. 2:20). One writer spoke of a certain
place near a monastery being full of the bones of babies. Thus,
we can see that the Roman Catholic Church propagates
fornication and promotes idolatry.

C. Built Up as a Religious Hierarchy

The Catholic Church is built up as a religious hierarchy
with the pope as the head. Under him are the cardinals, the
archbishops, the bishops, and the priests. The cardinals are
considered as the pope's cabinet members for his government.

The Catholic Church is a strong and powerful hierarchical organization.

D. The Great Harlot

Revelation 17 refers to the Roman Catholic Church as "the great harlot" and also refers to her as "Mystery, Babylon the Great, the mother of the harlots and the abominations of the earth" (vv. 1, 5). The Catholic Church is likened to a harlot who has adopted many heathen practices. Wherever the Catholic Church goes, it picks up the heathen practices of the local people. This is for the purpose of bringing these people into Catholicism.

E. Martyring the Saints and the Witnesses of Jesus

Revelation 17:6 reveals that the Catholic Church martyrs the saints and the witnesses of Jesus. History tells us that the Catholic Church, the Roman Church, has killed more saints than the Roman Empire did.

F. To Be Hated, Made Desolate, and Burned by Antichrist and His Ten Kings at the Beginning of the Great Tribulation

Eventually, the Catholic Church will be hated, made desolate, and burned by Antichrist and his ten kings at the beginning of the great tribulation. According to Revelation 17:16, Antichrist and his ten kings will make the Roman Church "desolate and naked," meaning that they will destroy her, rob her of her riches, and expose her; they will "eat her flesh," meaning that they will kill her members; and they will "burn her utterly with fire," meaning that they will annihilate her altogether.

In Revelation 14:8 an angel declares, "Fallen, fallen is Babylon the Great, who has made all the nations drink of the wine of the fury of her fornication!" This is the fall of religious Babylon. Religious Babylon is depicted in Revelation 17, and material Babylon is shown in Revelation 18. Religious Babylon will fall first at the beginning of the great tribulation, and material Babylon, the city of Rome, will fall at the end of the great tribulation.

G. To Overcome Such a Heretical Religion

To overcome such a heretical religion is by keeping the faith in Christ's divine and human person and all His works in His incarnation, crucifixion, resurrection, ascension, descension, and second appearing (2 Tim. 4:7c; Rev. 2:26). The way to overcome the Catholic heretical religion is by our faith in two things: the person of Christ and the work of Christ. We have to believe in Christ's person and in Christ's redemptive work according to the New Testament teaching from the first page to the last page. This is why we have to study the New Testament. We say a strong "amen" to the New Testament teaching that Jesus is both God, the complete God, and man, the perfect man. He was incarnated, He lived on earth as a human being for thirty-three and a half years, He died a vicarious, all-inclusive death, He resurrected, He ascended, and He descended. He is now in the heavens, and He will appear in His second coming. Because we have studied all these things with all their significances, such a deceiving church can never deceive us. We have a clear view concerning the teaching of the New Testament, the teaching of the apostles. This is the right way for us to keep our Christian faith.

III. PROTESTANTISM

A. Practicing the Works of the Nicolaitans, the Works of the Clergy in the Religious Hierarchy

Protestantism practices the works of the Nicolaitans, the works of the clergy in the religious hierarchy (Rev. 2:6). This is a strong sign of today's Protestant churches. In the Protestant churches there is a hierarchy with the clergy and the so-called laymen. A small number are clergy, and the majority are laymen. If we practice this, we are not in the recovery.

We have to consider whether or not we have the clergy and the laity in our meetings. We may not have the term *clergy,* but in actuality we may be building up the clergy. As long as we insist on keeping the system of one man speaking without the proper practice of every member of the church prophesying, we are building up the clergy.

Brother Nee saw the truth concerning the church meeting in mutuality revealed in 1 Corinthians 14 in 1937. His ministry on this is in the book entitled *The Normal Christian Church Life*. In 1948 he spoke concerning this again in the book entitled *Church Affairs*. But throughout the years, we did not find a way to replace the system of one man speaking with all of the saints prophesying. In 1984 I purposely went to Taiwan to restudy our situation in the recovery. In that study I was encouraged and strengthened by the Lord to pick up the practice of the church meetings revealed in 1 Corinthians 14.

Eventually, starting from the church in Taipei, we gave up the practice of one man speaking on the Lord's Day. Now we practice prophesying in the meetings by all the saints. We realize that we cannot do this in very large meetings, so the church in Taipei divided their three thousand attendants into a number of district meetings. Each district meeting has about fifty saints. Today many of the local churches are practicing the prophesying of all of the saints instead of the Lord's Day message meeting by one speaker.

In Revelation 2:6 the Lord Jesus says clearly that He hates the works of the Nicolaitans, the clergy-laity system (see note 6[1]—Recovery Version). We need to reject anything of this system. All of us should be the functioning members of the Body of Christ. Wherever clergy and laity are, hierarchy is being built up. Such a system changes the nature of the churches in the recovery.

B. Holding the Teaching of Balaam

Protestantism holds the teaching of Balaam, who put a stumbling block before the people of God, teaching people to accept idolatry and commit fornication (Rev. 2:14). Balaam was a Gentile prophet who spoke and taught the word of God for base gain, enticing God's people into fornication and idolatry (Num. 25:1-3; 31:16).

C. Holding the Teaching of the Nicolaitans

Protestantism also holds the teaching of the Nicolaitans to build up hierarchy and practice the system of clergy. In the seven epistles to the churches, the works of the Nicolaitans are mentioned first (Rev. 2:6). At first there was only the practice of the hierarchy with the clergy and laity. Later this practice became a teaching (v. 15). Today in Protestantism there is such a teaching. People are encouraged to dedicate themselves to the Lord, offering themselves to be preachers. Then they are sent to seminary, and after their graduation they become the clerical class. This is the practice and teaching in Protestantism.

D. Disregarding Christ's Headship in His Body

In today's Protestantism there is also a disregard for Christ's headship in His Body (Col. 1:18). In today's Protestant churches there is hardly any teaching concerning the Body of Christ and concerning Christ as the Head of the Body. In our teachings throughout the years, we have strongly stressed the building up of the Body of Christ and the headship of Christ.

E. Annulling the Functions of the Members in the Body of Christ

The Protestant churches annul the functions of the members in the Body of Christ. They maintain that to have one man speaking is better than to have all the saints function. They feel that having one man speaking keeps the meeting in a good order and ensures that a good word will be spoken to the attendants. They feel that a meeting left up to all the saints would end in chaos and confusion. By reading 1 Corinthians 14 we can see that Paul anticipated that the practice of all prophesying would not be so easy. This is why Paul charged them to do everything decently and in order (v. 40).

We like to be decent, but at the same time we do not like to be dead. Rather, we want to be living. I used to ask people, "What do you like better—Forest Lawn Cemetery or a playground?" A playground has very little order, but at Forest

Lawn Cemetery everything is in order. We do not want to have church meetings that are like a cemetery. Our church meetings need to be very living. The book of Psalms encourages us to make a joyful noise to the Lord (Psa. 100:1). We need such a joyful noise in our church meetings.

F. Keeping Most of the Church Meetings for the Service of the Clergy

In Protestantism most of the church meetings are kept for the service of the clergy, with nearly no meeting for the manifestation of the gifts of all the members of the Body for the organic building up of the Body of Christ in the unsearchable riches of Christ (cf. 1 Cor. 14:23a, 24, 26, 31, 3-5). Our meetings might be noisy, but out of the noise of all the saints the riches of Christ come out.

G. To Overcome Such a Dead and Dying Religion

We overcome such a dead and dying religion by the pneumatic Christ in His resurrection and by the bountiful supply of the all-inclusive Spirit (Phil. 3:10; 1:19b). On the one hand, Christ is the Son of God. On the other hand, He is the life-giving Spirit. First Corinthians 15:45b says Christ as the last Adam in the flesh became a life-giving Spirit through His resurrection. Thus, today He is the pneumatic Christ. By Christ as the pneumatic One and by the bountiful supply of the all-inclusive life-giving Spirit, we can overcome today's Protestantism.

CHAPTER FIVE

TO OVERCOME THE TREND
OF NOT KEEPING THE LORD'S WORD,
THE TIDE OF DENYING THE LORD'S NAME,
AND THE LUKEWARMNESS IN
THE LORD'S TESTIMONY

Scripture Reading: Rev. 3:7, 8b, 10-13, 14-21; 2:20; 3:2; 1 Pet. 1:7; Exo. 25:11; Rev. 1:20; 21:18; 1 John 2:27; 1 Cor. 15:45b; Eph. 3:8; Rev. 20:4, 6

OUTLINE

I. To overcome the trend of not keeping the Lord's word:
   A. In Catholicism the Lord's word is put aside and even locked; they keep the word of the prophetess Jezebel's teaching of heresies—Rev. 2:20.
   B. In Protestantism the Lord's word is unlocked, but it is not kept with absoluteness—Rev. 3:2.
   C. In the recovery the Lord's word is kept absolutely, even as much as by the "little power" that we can afford—Rev. 3:8b.
II. To overcome the tide of denying the Lord's name:
   A. The Lord's word is the Lord's expression; the Lord's name denotes the Lord's person.
   B. In Protestantism there is a strong tide of denying the Lord's name by replacing it with many other names, such as Episcopalian, Lutheran, Methodist, Baptist, Presbyterian, etc.
   C. In the recovery the Lord's name, Jesus Christ, is unique, without any replacement.
   D. The reward for keeping the Lord's word and not denying the Lord's name:

    1. To be kept out of the hour of trial, which is about to come on the whole inhabited earth, to try them who dwell on the earth—Rev. 3:10.

    2. To receive the crown—Rev. 3:11.

    3. To be made a pillar (for the building of God) in the temple of God, upon which are written the name of God, the name of the city of God, the New Jerusalem, and the new name of Christ—Rev. 3:12.

III. To overcome the lukewarmness in the Lord's testimony—Rev. 3:15-16; 12:17b:

    A. To hate and abhor the pride and boast of being wealthy and rich in the vain doctrinal knowledge—Rev. 3:17a.

    B. To realize our spiritual condition—wretched (because of the pride and boast of vanity), miserable (because of the poverty, nakedness, and blindness), poor (in the experience of Christ and in the reality of God's economy), blind (lacking spiritual insight in the genuine spiritual things), and naked (without the covering of Christ as the subjective righteousness)—Rev. 3:17b.

    C. To buy at a cost—Rev. 3:18:

        1. Refined gold, signifying the living faith (1 Pet. 1:7) for the gaining of the Triune God embodied in Christ as the pure gold (Exo. 25:11), that we may be the pure golden lampstand (Rev. 1:20) for the building of the golden New Jerusalem (Rev. 21:18) to make us truly rich.

        2. White garments, signifying Christ lived out of us as our subjective righteousness to cover our nakedness.

        3. Eyesalve, signifying the anointing life-giving Spirit (1 John 2:27; 1 Cor. 15:45b), that we may have the sight to see the divine and spiritual things for the healing of our spiritual blindness.

    D. To open ourselves to the Lord, who is shut outside the door of the church—Rev. 3:20a.

E. The reward:
   1. To feast with the Lord, signifying the rich and full enjoyment of the unsearchable riches of Christ—Rev. 3:20b; Eph. 3:8.
   2. To participate in sitting with Christ on His throne for the fellowship in His kingship in authority—Rev. 3:21; 20:4, 6.

By reading the Lord's epistles to the churches in Revelation 2 and 3, we can see what we need to overcome. The epistle to Ephesus shows us that we need to overcome the leaving of Christ as our first love that we may eat Him as the tree of life to be the lampstand, corporately shining out the divine light (2:4-5, 7). The epistle to Smyrna shows that we need to overcome persecution, comprising tribulation, poverty, trial, imprisonment, and the slander of the deformed religion of Satan (2:9-10a). Furthermore, we have to overcome the worldliness of Pergamos so that we can eat the Lord Jesus as the hidden manna for our nourishment, for our supply, and for our support so that we can become a white stone, justified and approved by the Lord for His divine building (2:13, 17b). Instead of being worldly, we need to become the enjoyers and eaters of the Lord Jesus in a particular, hidden way. This will make us precious material for His building. In order for us to participate in His divine building, we have to be rescued and delivered from worldliness.

We have also seen that we need to overcome the spiritual death of Sardis (3:1-2). The crucial point concerning those in the church in Sardis is that they are dead and dying. While they have a name that they are living, actually they are dead. To overcome spiritual death we need to be watchful and establish the things of life, which are about to die. We must overcome so that we are not defiled with the stain of spiritual death (vv. 2, 4).

We have also seen that we need to overcome the three deformed religions—Judaism, which is referred to as the "synagogue of Satan"; Catholicism, seen with the church in Thyatira; and Protestantism, seen mainly with the church in Sardis. We can overcome these "isms" by giving the preeminence to Christ. We should tell the Lord that in our dealings with these "isms," we want to give the preeminence to Him. We need to give Him the preeminence in everything, in the small things and in the big things. In Revelation 2 and 3, the Lord called us to be overcomers. The overcoming in these two chapters is not mainly to overcome in our daily life but mainly to overcome the big things concerning the deformed religions. We have to be those who overcome degraded Christianity.

In this chapter we want to see that we need to overcome the trend of not keeping the Lord's word, the tide of denying the Lord's name, and the lukewarmness in the Lord's testimony.

I. TO OVERCOME THE TREND OF NOT KEEPING THE LORD'S WORD

The church has been in this world for over nineteen centuries. On the day of Pentecost, three thousand were saved and baptized to begin the church life (Acts 2:41). They all received the outpouring of the Holy Spirit. Then they began to meet in their homes, and they were together to continue in the fellowship and the teaching of the apostles (v. 42). The teaching of the apostles is the Lord's word. They continued day and night in two things—in the fellowship and in the teaching of the apostles. No doubt, they were very strict in keeping the word of God.

That was wonderful, but since that day this kind of diligent, strict keeping of the word of God has become loose. How many Christians today keep the word of God strictly, continuously, and daily? It is difficult to find anyone that keeps the Lord's word in such a way. Today among the Christians there is a trend of not keeping the Lord's word. They have the Bible, but the Bible remains mostly on their bookshelf. Many of them do not even bring their Bible when they attend their Sunday morning service.

A. In Catholicism the Lord's Word Being Put Aside and Even Locked

In Catholicism the Lord's word is put aside and even locked. Those in Catholicism maintain that the so-called laymen are not qualified and do not have the capacity, the ability, to understand the holy Word. Thus, they feel that they should let the pope, the cardinals, the archbishops, the bishops, and the priests study the Bible, understand it, and interpret it. To them what matters is not what the Bible says but what the pope says, what their church says. According to

Revelation 2:20 they keep the word of the prophetess
Jezebel's teaching of heresies. Jezebel, typifying today's
Catholic Church, is the woman mentioned in Matthew 13:33
who leavened the entire teaching concerning Christ. This
is the condition of Catholicism toward God's word.

B. In Protestantism the Lord's Word Being Unlocked but Not Being Kept with Absoluteness

In Protestantism the Lord's word is unlocked, but it is not
kept with absoluteness (Rev. 3:2). From Martin Luther's time,
the Bible became unlocked, but it was not open to people's
understanding. Today it is not kept with absoluteness. It is
very rare to meet Christians who are fearful and trembling
in dealing with the Word of God.

Many times Christians will say, "I know what the Bible
says, but...." There is always a "but" in their attitude toward
what God's Word says. We should not say "but" to the Word of
God. This is a big offense to the Lord. The Lord says, "Deny
yourself" (Matt. 16:24). We say, "*But* I cannot afford to do it."
The Lord says, "Love one another" (John 13:34). We say, "Lord
Jesus, I want to love all Your believers, *but* some of them are
not lovable." We need to be corrected by the Spirit not to say
"but" to the Lord. Instead, we should say, "Yes, Lord."

We have a hymn in our hymnal which says, "To the foe
my word is always, 'No,' / To the Father it is 'Yes'" (*Hymns,*
#880). We have to learn to say "yes" to the Father and "no"
to the devil all the time. But often our experience is the oppo-
site of this. We say "no" to the Father and "yes" to Satan.
When the sisters see something on sale in the newspaper,
there is a struggle within them. Something within is urging
them to go buy it, and something within is telling them not
to go. Thus, they have to decide what to say. Will they say
"no" to Satan and "yes" to the Father? They may say to the
Lord, "Lord, I ask You to give me the freedom to go this
one time. I will never do it again." All of us have this same
"illness." We read the Bible, but do we keep the word of the
Bible? We should be those who keep the Lord's word with
absoluteness.

C. In the Recovery the Lord's Word Being Kept Absolutely

In the recovery the Lord's word is kept absolutely, even by the "little power" that we can afford (Rev. 3:8b). The Lord commended the church in Philadelphia by saying that they kept His word even with the little power that they had. Today on this earth it is difficult to meet one who is faithful to the word of God every day and even every moment. We have to overcome today's trend of not keeping the Lord's word.

In the recovery the Lord's word is kept absolutely. If there is not such an absolute keeping of the word of God with us, we are not in the recovery. We have to keep the Lord's word even according to the "little power" that we can afford. We should keep the Lord's word as much as we can. I have learned from the Bible and also from my experience that the Lord is fair. The Lord would never "over request" anything from us. He would never request anything that we cannot afford to do. We should be at peace, and say "yes" to Him all the time.

I learned the lesson of always saying "yes" to the Lord, but after I said "yes," I said, "Lord, I like to keep Your word, but You know I am weak." The Lord then rebuked me by saying, "Don't tell me you are weak. I know you are weak, but I am your grace, and My grace is sufficient for you to keep My word." We need to return in a full way to the Lord's word, and keep the word absolutely by the Lord as our all-sufficient grace.

II. TO OVERCOME THE TIDE OF DENYING THE LORD'S NAME

Today there is a trend of not keeping the Lord's word, and there is also a tide of denying the Lord's name. Today's Protestant churches have taken many names other than the name of the Lord Jesus Christ.

A. The Lord's Word Being the Lord's Expression, and the Lord's Name Denoting the Lord's Person

The Lord's word is the Lord's expression, and the Lord's name denotes the Lord's person. The recovered church not only has returned in a full way to the Lord's word but also has abandoned all names other than the name of the Lord Jesus Christ.

B. The Strong Tide of Denying the Lord's Name in Protestantism

In Protestantism there is a strong tide of denying the Lord's name by replacing it with many other names, such as Lutheran, Methodist, Baptist, Presbyterian, etc. Many Christians say that they go to the Lutheran church, the Methodist church, or the Presbyterian church. There is also the Episcopalian church, the Anglican church, the Church of England. The word *Episcopalian* is from the Latin word *episcopus,* meaning bishop. The Church of England is a state church under the rule of bishops.

We can see that Protestantism has replaced the unique name of Christ with many other names. Today it is very convenient for people to set up a church and give a name to it. There are many Chinese churches in California with many names other than the name of Christ. One denomination calls itself the Taiwan Presbyterian Church. Another one is called the Taiwan Gospel Church. To denominate the church by taking any name other than the Lord's is spiritual fornication. The church, as the pure virgin espoused to Christ (2 Cor. 11:2), should have no name other than her Husband's. All other names are an abomination in the eyes of God.

It is serious for a woman to take another name besides that of her husband. If a woman is married to Mr. Jones, she should not call herself Mrs. Smith. When believers designate themselves with a name other than Christ's name, this indicates that they are taking someone or something other than Christ as their Husband. If Mrs. Jones calls herself Mrs. Smith, this means that she has two husbands. The church is a chaste virgin espoused to Christ, so the church is the wife of Christ, and Christ is the Husband. A wife should have only one husband, and her husband's name becomes her name. From the day of her wedding, she belongs to her husband, and her last name must be her husband's name.

But today the so-called churches use other names, names replacing Christ. This is a big insult to Christ.

In the early 1800s, some brothers raised up by the Lord in England dropped all these divisive names. They would keep only one name, that is, the name of the Lord Jesus Christ. Eventually, others did not know how to denominate them, so they called them "The Brethren." This is because they called themselves "brothers," or "brethren."

When we were raised up by the Lord in China, we realized that we should not denominate ourselves with any name. A denomination is a group of Christians who have denominated themselves with a certain name such as Lutheran, Wesleyan, Anglican, Presbyterian, Baptist, etc. They do not realize that this is an insult to Christ. Strictly speaking, it is spiritual fornication. If our Husband's name is Christ, and we take the name Lutheran, this means that we are taking another husband.

Furthermore, the many names taken in today's Protestantism strongly imply divisions. The recovered church has only the unique name of the Lord Jesus Christ. Every group taking a name other than Christ is a division. Christ is unique and is not divided, but all the different names are very divisive. In 1 Corinthians Paul said, "Each of you says, I am of Paul, and I of Apollos, and I of Cephas, and I of Christ. Is Christ divided?" (1:12-13a). This is exactly the same as saying "I am a Lutheran," "I am a Wesleyan," "I am a Presbyterian," "I am an Episcopalian," etc. All such designations should be condemned and rejected. Furthermore, to say "I am of Christ" in the way of excluding the apostles and their teachings or of excluding other believers is as divisive as to say "I am of" this or that. The divisions can be eliminated and terminated only by taking Christ as the unique center among all the believers. Brother Watchman Nee in his book *Further Talks on the Church Life* said that those in the denominations may say that they love one another, but they "shake hands over the fences" of their denominations (see pp. 95-102). We must overcome to tear down all the fences so that we can have the fellowship of the Body of Christ in oneness.

C. In the Recovery the Lord's Name, Jesus Christ, Being Unique, without Any Replacement

In the recovery the Lord's name, Jesus Christ, is unique, without any replacement. The church in the Lord's recovery does not take a name. We are simply the church. The moon is just the moon. It is not designated with another name. The church should not be designated. If we designate the church, it becomes a denomination, a division. Denominations cut the Body of Christ into pieces. Any name of any denomination is a divisive and evil thing. We need to overcome the tide of denying the Lord's name. To take another name besides that of Christ is abominable in the eyes of God because it is spiritual fornication.

D. The Reward for Keeping the Lord's Word and Not Denying the Lord's Name

Now we want to see the reward for keeping the Lord's word and not denying the Lord's name.

1. To Be Kept Out of the Hour of Trial

The first reward to the overcomers is to be kept out of the hour of trial, which is about to come on the whole inhabited earth, to try them who dwell on the earth (Rev. 3:10). *Trial* here undoubtedly denotes the great tribulation (Matt. 24:21), which is about to come on the whole inhabited earth. The Lord Jesus promised the Philadelphian overcomers that before the tribulation begins, He will take them away. This indicates that the saints who keep the Lord's word and do not deny the Lord's name will be raptured before the great tribulation. This is a great promise and a great reward.

2. To Receive the Crown

The overcomers will receive the crown (Rev. 3:11), which indicates their victory and authority. In New Testament usage, a crown always denotes a prize that is in addition to salvation (Rev. 2:10; 3:11; James 1:12; 2 Tim. 4:8; 1 Pet. 5:4; 1 Cor. 9:25).

3. To Be Made a Pillar (for the Building of God) in the Temple of God

The overcomers who keep the Lord's word and do not deny His name will be made pillars (for the building of God) in the temple of God, upon which are written the name of God, the name of the city of God, the New Jerusalem, and the new name of Christ (Rev. 3:12). In Revelation 2:17 the overcomer will become a transformed stone for God's building. In 3:12 the overcomer will become a pillar built into the temple of God. Because he is built into God's building, he shall by no means go out anymore. This promise, as a prize to the overcomer, will be fulfilled in the millennial kingdom.

The pillar in the temple of God will bear the name of God, the name of the New Jerusalem, and also the new name of Christ. This indicates that the overcomer is possessed by and is one with God, the New Jerusalem, and Christ. This also indicates that the overcomer belongs to these three names. When someone purchases a new Bible, he may sign his name in it. His name indicates that this Bible is his possession. The overcomers will be the possession of God, the possession of Christ, and the possession of the New Jerusalem. Actually, they are a part of the New Jerusalem, so they bear the name of the New Jerusalem.

The overcomers bear the new name of Christ. This does not mean that Christ has a new name. It means that Christ will be experienced by these overcomers in a new way. Thus, the very Christ they are experiencing is new to them. If we would make up our minds to take the overcoming way, we will experience Christ in a new way, and Christ will become new to us. Our Owner will be God, the New Jerusalem, and the new Christ.

To many of us Christ is old, not new. At the beginning of our Christian life, Christ was new to us, but gradually that new Christ became old to us. We have Christ, but is Christ new to us? Mostly our experience of Christ is too old. It may be that our experience of Him is the same as it was ten years ago. He is old to us. But if we make the decision to be an overcomer in this age, we will have the sense that Christ is so fresh and new. We will enjoy Him as God's new mercies refreshing us every morning (Lam. 3:22-23).

Thus, those who overcome the trend of not keeping the Lord's word and the tide of denying His name will be raptured before the great tribulation, will receive the crown, and will be made a pillar for the building of God, having the name of God, the name of the New Jerusalem, and the new name of Christ.

III. TO OVERCOME THE LUKEWARMNESS IN THE LORD'S TESTIMONY

We also need to overcome the lukewarmness in the Lord's testimony (Rev. 3:15-16; 12:17b). To be lukewarm is to be neither hot nor cold.

A. To Hate and Abhor the Pride and Boast of Being Wealthy and Rich in the Vain Doctrinal Knowledge

To overcome lukewarmness, we have to hate and abhor our pride. We may be too proud and content with our present situation. We also have to hate and abhor the boast of being wealthy and rich in the vain doctrinal knowledge (Rev. 3:17a). We may have been in the recovery for a number of years, and during this time we may think that we have accumulated many truths. We may think that we are wealthy, but we may be wealthy only in vain doctrinal knowledge. We can know doctrines but not have the spiritual insight to comprehend the genuine reality in God's economy. We have to hate this because such knowledge is vain and meaningless.

B. To Realize Our Spiritual Condition

In order to overcome lukewarmness, we also have to realize our spiritual condition. According to Revelation 3:17, the condition of those in Laodicea was wretched (because of the pride and boast of vanity), miserable (because of poverty, nakedness, and blindness), poor (in the experience of Christ and in the reality of God's economy), blind (lacking spiritual insight in the genuine spiritual things), and naked (without the covering of Christ as the subjective righteousness). We have to realize our spiritual condition and have a new start in our spiritual life.

C. To Buy at a Cost Gold, White Garments, and Eyesalve

Buying requires the paying of a price. The degraded recovered church must pay a price for gold, white garments, and eyesalve, which she desperately needs (Rev. 3:18).

1. Refined Gold, Signifying the Living Faith

We need to buy the refined gold, which signifies the living faith (1 Pet. 1:7) for the gaining of the Triune God embodied in Christ as the pure gold (Exo. 25:11), that we may be the pure golden lampstand (Rev. 1:20) for the building of the golden New Jerusalem (Rev. 21:18) to make us truly rich. Our living faith is gold, and this very Christ embodying God is also gold. Actually, our faith and Christ are one, so they are the same gold.

In the New Testament, our faith, the living faith, is a person, and that person is Christ. This is why we have to look unto Him, pray to Him, have fellowship with Him, and read His Word. The more we read His Word and listen to His word, the more the living Christ will be inwardly unveiled to us, and this inward Christ will be the spontaneous faith to us. Faith is not a mere action but a living person, living in us and acting in us. The living faith which is Christ Himself is the gold which we have to buy.

2. White Garments, Signifying Christ Lived Out of Us as Our Subjective Righteousness to Cover Our Nakedness

We also need to buy white garments, signifying Christ lived out of us as our subjective righteousness to cover our nakedness. How much do we have Christ as our subjective righteousness, which is Christ Himself living out from within us? We all have to confess our shortcoming in this matter. We need the Lord Himself lived out of us as our white garments for the covering of our nakedness.

3. Eyesalve, Signifying the Anointing
Life-giving Spirit, That We May Have the Sight
to See the Divine and Spiritual Things for
the Healing of Our Spiritual Blindness

We also need to buy the eyesalve, signifying the anointing life-giving Spirit (1 John 2:27; 1 Cor. 15:45b). This is so that we may have the sight to see the divine and spiritual things for the healing of our spiritual blindness. All of us need to pay the price for these three things: the refined gold, the white garments, and the eyesalve.

D. To Open Ourselves to the Lord,
Who Is Shut outside the Door of the Church

In order to overcome lukewarmness, we need to open ourselves to the Lord, who is shut outside the door of the lukewarm church. Revelation 3:20 reveals that the Lord is outside the door of the church in Laodicea. Thus, He is not within the church in Laodicea but is outside knocking at the door. The door is the door of the church, but the door is opened by individual believers. To the one who opens the door, the Lord will enter into him to feast with him. We should have the assurance that every morning our door is wide open to the Lord so that He can come in to dine with us, to feast with us.

E. The Reward

1. To Feast with the Lord,
Signifying the Rich and Full Enjoyment
of the Unsearchable Riches of Christ

The overcomers will be rewarded by Christ. They will feast with the Lord, signifying the rich and full enjoyment of the unsearchable riches of Christ (Rev. 3:20b; Eph. 3:8). When we open to the Lord, He and we will enjoy each other. Then His presence becomes our feast, and our presence becomes His feast. Thus, we dine with each other, feasting together. This is the practical and full enjoyment of Christ in our daily life. Every day we should have such a feast.

2. To Participate in Sitting with Christ on His Throne for the Fellowship in His Kingship in Authority

Eventually, the overcomers will participate in sitting with Christ as the King on His throne for the fellowship, the participation, in His kingship as His co-kings in authority to rule over all the nations (Rev. 3:21; 20:4, 6).

We can see from this fellowship that we all need to aspire to be the overcomers. We have to overcome big things like the three deformed religions and small things like our attitude and the way that we dress. When a husband loses his temper with his wife, at that moment he is no longer an overcomer but a failure in his daily life. Day by day we have to overcome in all the small things.

We should not say "no" to the Lord and "yes" to Satan. We should always practice to say "yes" to the Lord and "no" to Satan. We should say "no" to all of the "isms." We should say "no" to the denominations, to the exalting of all the names other than the unique name of Christ. For a Christian to take another name besides the name of Christ is a shame and an insult to Him. We must make a definite decision to take the Lord's way, the way of being an overcomer. We must overcome the trend of not keeping the Lord's word, the tide of denying the Lord's name, and the lukewarmness in the Lord's testimony.

Chapter Six

THE FINAL CONSUMMATION OF THE OVERCOMERS

Scripture Reading: Rev. 6:9-11; 12:1-6; 14:1-5; 15:2-4; 13:7a; 11:3-12; 2 Cor. 5:10; Rev. 11:18c; 19:7-9; 17:14; 19:14; Joel 3:11; Rev. 19:19-21; 11:15; 20:4, 6; Matt. 5:20; 19:23-30; 1 Cor. 6:9-10; Gal. 5:19-21; Eph. 5:3-5; 2 Pet. 1:11; Matt. 19:28; Rev. 22:3b; 2:26-27; 12:5; 2:7; Matt. 13:43; Dan. 12:2-3, 13; Rev. 21:1-3, 9-12, 14; 22:17

OUTLINE

I. The composition of the overcomers:
   A. The overcomers crying to the Lord for His avenging at the fifth seal, comprising all the martyrs from Abel to those before the fifth seal—Rev. 6:9-11.
   B. The man-child born of the universal woman—Rev. 12:1-5:
      1. Comprising the martyrs who cry at the fifth seal and the additional martyrs before the great tribulation.
      2. To be resurrected and raptured to the throne of God before the three and a half years of the great tribulation—vv. 4b-6.
   C. The one hundred forty-four thousand living overcomers raptured before the great tribulation to Mount Zion in the heavens before God's throne as firstfruits to God and to the Lamb—Rev. 14:1-5.
   D. The martyrs in the great tribulation under the persecution of Antichrist resurrected and raptured to stand on the glassy sea close to the end of the great tribulation—Rev. 15:2-4; 13:7a.

E. The two witnesses martyred, resurrected, and raptured to the heavens in the cloud at the close of the great tribulation—Rev. 11:3-12.

II. The final consummation of the overcomers:
  A. To be manifested as a corporate overcomer after their raptures.
  B. To be rewarded at the judgment seat of Christ— 2 Cor. 5:10; Rev. 11:18c.
  C. To be the bride married to the Lamb—Rev. 19:7-9.
  D. To be the army of the Lamb—Rev. 17:14; 19:14:
    1. To come as the mighty ones with Christ—Joel 3:11.
    2. To defeat, with Christ, Antichrist and his armies—Rev. 19:19-21.
    3. To close the great tribulation and the present age.
  E. To bring in the kingdom of God and of Christ— Rev. 11:15; 20:4, 6.
  F. To inherit the kingdom of God and of Christ in the fuller enjoyment of the eternal life—Matt. 5:20; 19:23-30; 1 Cor. 6:9-10; Gal. 5:19-21; Eph. 5:3-5; 2 Pet. 1:11:
    1. To be co-kings with Christ—Rev. 20:4, 6; Matt. 19:28.
    2. To be priests of God and of Christ—Rev. 20:6; 22:3b.
    3. To enjoy the ruling authority over the nations— Rev. 2:26-27; 12:5.
  G. To be the New Jerusalem, as the bride of Christ for one thousand years, in its initial and fresh stage:
    1. As the present Paradise of God in the millennial kingdom—Rev. 2:7.
    2. To shine forth like the sun in the kingdom of their Father in the heavenly part of the millennium—Matt. 13:43; cf. Dan. 12:2-3, 13.
  H. To consummate and complete the New Jerusalem in full, as the tabernacle of God and the wife of Christ in the new heaven and new earth for eternity—Rev. 21:1-2, 9-10:

    1. With the addition of all the saints perfected for their maturity in the divine life through the discipline in the kingdom age—Rev. 21:2, 12, 14.

    2. For the eternal expression, to its fullest extent, of the processed Triune God in, with, and through all the regenerated, transformed, and glorified tripartite saints in eternity—Rev. 21:10-11.

I. To consummate finally the Triune God's eternal economy in Christ through the consummated Spirit—Rev. 22:17.

J. To participate in the fullest enjoyment of the processed and consummated Triune God in the fellowship with all the redeemed and glorified saints forever and ever.

In this chapter we want to see the final consummation of the overcomers. If we read the Bible thoroughly, we can see that the overcomers are the life-line, the pulse, of the entire Bible. The first overcomer among God's people was Abel (Gen. 4:2-8). The Lord Jesus in Matthew 23:35 referred to the martyrdom of Abel, indicating that he was the first overcomer. Starting from Abel the Lord has continued to gain overcomers to ultimately consummate His economy and bring in the kingdom of Christ and of God (Rev. 11:15).

We have pointed out that the book of Revelation is on the overcomers and the New Jerusalem. The overcomers have a strong issue, and this issue is the conclusion of the divine revelation. The New Jerusalem is the ending, the conclusion, and the totality of the divine revelation in the sixty-six books of the Bible.

The crucial items in Revelation 21 and 22 concerning the New Jerusalem were already mentioned previously in the Bible. The most striking point in the New Jerusalem is the tree of life, which was mentioned at the beginning of the Bible (Gen. 2:9). If there were no tree of life in the holy city, there would be no food for God's redeemed to live on. The tree of life is the centrality and universality of the holy city.

The New Jerusalem is actually a high mountain with a height of twelve thousand stadia. The city is a cube with the length, breadth, and height all being equal (Rev. 21:16). The Holy of Holies in both the tabernacle and the temple was a cube, being equal in length, breadth, and height (Exo. 26:2-8; 1 Kings 6:20). Hence, the New Jerusalem being a cube signifies that the entire city will be the Holy of Holies. In it, all God's redeemed ones will serve and worship God, will see and touch God's presence, and will live and dwell in God's presence for eternity. The center of the New Jerusalem is the tree of life for the feeding and nourishing of the entire city.

Now we need to consider how one tree could be available to feed the entire city. The tree of life is not like a pine tree. Because a pine tree is so tall, it is not available to us. The tree of life is a vine tree. Christ is the vine tree (John 15:1) and He is the life (John 14:6a), so He is the tree of life. That the one tree of life grows on the two sides of the river of water of life (Rev. 22:2) signifies that the tree of life is a vine that spreads and proceeds along the flow of the water of life for God's people to receive and enjoy. A pine tree grows high, but a vine tree spreads. If we want to eat the tree of life, we do not need a "ladder," because this tree is a vine tree so available for us to eat.

The river of water of life in the New Jerusalem is within the one golden street (Rev. 22:1). The tree of life grows in and alongside the river of water of life, which spirals down the mountain to reach all twelve gates of the city. The tree of life as a great vine is the available food, the nourishment, for God's redeemed in eternity, so it is the life-pulse of the New Jerusalem. I went to England in 1958, and someone took me to see a big vine tree called the Queen's vine. But this vine is very small in comparison with the vine that I have seen. I have seen the great vine tree, the tree of life, in the New Jerusalem. The Lord Jesus said that He was the true vine (John 15:1). He is the vine tree and we are the branches (v. 5). He is the centrality and universality of God's economy, and God's economy consummates in the New Jerusalem.

The divine revelation in the Bible, beginning from God's creation in Genesis 1, concludes with two long chapters, Revelation 21—22. In these two chapters is the New Jerusalem as a great and strong sign of God's economy. The centrality and universality of this holy city is the tree of life, the greatest vine in the universe. This vine comprises our God, our Lord, our Master, our Father, our Lord Jesus Christ, and us. We are a part of this vine because we are the branches.

In Genesis 2 we see the tree of life, and after all the ages the tree of life is still present in the New Jerusalem. The Triune God embodied in Christ was the tree of life at the beginning, but at the end of the Bible, the tree of life is spreading throughout the holy city. Thus, the Bible starts with the tree of life and ends with the tree of life.

In Genesis 2 along with the tree of life, there is also a river. This river had four heads and flowed toward the four directions of the earth (vv. 10-14). Then in the New Jerusalem, there is a river in which the tree of life grows. Thus, there is a river at the beginning and end of the Bible. At the flow of the river in Genesis 2 there were gold, bdellium (a kind of pearl) and onyx stone, a precious stone (vv. 11-12). Then at the end of the Bible, the holy city is built with gold, pearls, and precious stones (Rev. 21:18-21). There is the same picture at the beginning and end of the Bible of the tree of life with a flowing river issuing in gold, pearls, and precious stones.

In Genesis 2 the material was just lying there, but at the end of the Bible the gold, pearls, and precious stones are built into a city. In the beginning there was a garden created by God, but at the end the garden becomes a city. The city is something created by God which has been transformed and built up. The New Jerusalem is a building with gold, pearls, and precious stones. The beginning and end of the Bible reflect each other. The New Jerusalem as a city has twelve gates, and at the end of the book of Ezekiel, there is also a city by the name of Jerusalem with twelve gates (48:31-35). This shows us that on the one hand, the New Jerusalem is new; on the other hand, it is ancient.

The entire Bible is a revelation and a record of God's economy, and God's economy is consummated in the New Jerusalem. The New Jerusalem was something in God's heart in eternity past. This city is God's desire, God's good pleasure. I believe that God saw the New Jerusalem in eternity past. When He looked at that, He was happy.

When I was in Chefoo over fifty years ago, I had a dream of building a large meeting hall for the ministry of the word. This dream could be considered as my economy, my heart's desire, my good pleasure. But eventually China was taken over by the communists, and I did not see the completion of my dream to have such a hall. Then I was sent from mainland China to Taiwan. In Taiwan we were not able to have a big meeting hall according to the one I envisioned. I began to minister in the United States in 1962, and we eventually moved to Anaheim in 1974. In Anaheim we were able to acquire two and a half acres of land to build a meeting hall according to my dream in Chefoo many years earlier. Today's hall in Anaheim had been in my thoughts many years before it was built.

God also had a dream, and that dream was to have the New Jerusalem, a built up city, as the consummation of His economy. At the beginning of the Bible, we see the tree of life, a flowing river, and precious materials. At the end of the Bible, we also see the tree of life, a flowing river, and precious materials built into a city according to God's economy. By this we can see how consistent the Bible is. It was written by more than forty writers within a period of about fifteen hundred years. Apparently Genesis is much different from Matthew, and Matthew is much different from Revelation. It may seem that the sixty-six books of the Bible are independently different. Actually, the very intrinsic essence of the Bible is consistent. It is consistent in one thing—the New Jerusalem.

The New Jerusalem comprises the Triune God and His chosen and redeemed people. The Triune God has gone through a wonderful process. In eternity past He was God, having only divinity, but one day according to His economy, He became a man. This is because His economy, His blueprint, shows that He wants to be one with man.

He took the step to be incarnated four thousand years after Adam was created. From Adam to Abraham was two thousand years, and from Abraham to Christ was two thousand years. The very Triune God became a man. He did not become a man magically. His incarnation was altogether according to the principle He had ordained in His creation. For a man to be brought into existence, he must be conceived and remain in the womb for nine months. Then he is born and grows into manhood. This is the way Jesus came. He was conceived in the womb of a virgin, and He was born out of her womb. Then He passed through boyhood and entered into manhood. He lived on this earth for thirty-three and a half years.

What a wonder that the almighty, infinite, eternal Triune God would enter into the womb of the virgin Mary to be born of her and to be a typical man to live, walk, and work on earth for thirty-three and a half years! The very almighty God who created the heavens and the earth with millions of items became a man and lived on this earth as a little man for thirty-three and a half years to be persecuted, to be despised, to be rejected, to be hated, and to be abhorred by His creatures. This means that He has gone through a process, and through His process He has been consummated to be the processed and consummated Triune God. Such a God is included in the New Jerusalem, and we are there mingled with Him as one entity.

The New Jerusalem is a great sign because the book of Revelation is a book of signs. Revelation 1:1 says that the revelation of this book is made known by signs, symbols with spiritual significance. The seven lampstands are signs, signifying the seven churches (1:20). The Lamb signifies Christ as the redeeming God (5:6). The Lord Jesus is not a literal lamb with a tail and four legs. The Lamb is a sign. In the same way, the entire New Jerusalem is a sign, signifying the ultimate consummation of God's economy. We need signs because a picture is better than a thousand words. It is very difficult to describe what a person looks like, so the best way is to have a photo of that person. The New Jerusalem in the Bible is a "photo" of all the secrets, all the mysteries, of God's economy.

In His economy God would not accomplish anything merely by Himself. In His economy He has determined to do everything in and with humanity. God's old creation was carried out in six days, but to accomplish His economy to gain the New Jerusalem takes God at least seven thousand years. It takes God so long because He needs man. He needs human cooperation.

We were caught by the Lord for the carrying out of His economy. Many years ago I was endeavoring to gain the best education. I knew that, humanly speaking, education was my future. One afternoon in my home town I heard a young lady preach the gospel in a large meeting place to an audience of over one thousand people. I was nineteen years old and she was twenty-five years old. I was very curious to hear what she would speak. In that meeting, as a young ambitious man, I was caught, "hooked," by the Lord Jesus. As I was walking back home from the meeting, I consecrated my entire life and future to the Lord. I told Him that I wanted to go throughout the villages to preach Christ. I was "hooked" by Him.

While this enterprising Triune God is on the way to accomplish His economy, He passes through the earth, and here and there, there and here, He gained us for His heart's desire. He redeemed us, washed us, justified us, and reconciled us to Himself. He regenerated us by entering into us in a hidden way. When we heard the gospel, repented of our sins, and believed into Christ, we were not conscious that God came inside of us. But this is what happened when we were regenerated. From that time onward, He has been sanctifying us, renewing us, transforming us, and conforming us to the image of the firstborn Son of God. As we are in this process, we are waiting for and expecting the time when He will come to glorify us. When He glorifies us, He will bring our entire being into His glory to make us absolutely the same as He is in every way. Of course, we do not and will not have His Godhead for people to worship us. We are not to be worshipped by anyone, but we do have God's life (1 John 5:12) and God's nature (2 Pet. 1:4). We are holy as He is, spiritual as He is, and divine as He is. We regenerated Christians are both human and divine. As the human and divine ones, we all become a part of the New Jerusalem. This is the way God takes to consummate His economy, to complete His wonderful masterpiece, the New Jerusalem.

The divine design and composition of the New Jerusalem is marvelous. Gold signifies God in His divine nature, and the entire mount of the New Jerusalem is gold (Rev. 21:18). God in His nature is the base for the building up of the New Jerusalem. The city is also built with precious stones. The foundation of the city is twelve layers of precious stones (vv. 19-20). On these twelve layers are the twelve names of the twelve apostles of the Lamb (v. 14). The twelve layers of the foundation have the appearance of a rainbow, signifying that the city is built upon and secured by God's faithfulness in keeping His covenant (Gen. 9:8-17) and that the foundation of the city is trustworthy and reliable.

The city also has twelve pearl gates (Rev. 21:21). Pearls are produced by oysters in the waters of death. When an oyster is wounded by a grain of sand, it secretes its life-juice around the grain of sand, making it into a precious pearl. This depicts

Christ as the living One coming into the death waters, being wounded by us, and secreting His life over us to make us into precious pearls for the building of God's eternal expression.

The New Jerusalem is not only a composition but also a constitution of God and man. God has been constituted into man, and man has been constituted into Him. God dwells in man and man dwells in Him. God and man coinhere, that is, they mutually indwell each other. Eventually, the New Jerusalem is the mingling of God and man. In the whole universe, there will be a big cube, the New Jerusalem, which is the mingling of divinity with humanity.

I. THE COMPOSITION OF THE OVERCOMERS

The composition of the overcomers is the categories, the different kinds, of overcomers.

A. The Overcomers Crying to the Lord for His Avenging at the Fifth Seal, Comprising All the Martyrs from Abel to Those before the Fifth Seal

Revelation 6:9-11 reveals the overcomers crying to the Lord for His avenging at the fifth seal. This group of overcomers comprises all the martyrs from Abel to those before the fifth seal. Today we are in the first four seals. The fifth seal has not come yet, but it may come soon. In the Old Testament times, there were a number of martyrs who sacrificed themselves to die for the Lord's interest (Heb. 11:35-38). They were overcomers in the Old Testament. Then in the New Testament, from the time of the early apostles to our time there have been many more martyrs. Throughout the approximately nineteen centuries of church history, many faithful saints have been martyred. Some were not martyred physically but psychologically. They were martyred in their soul, their psyche, their emotion, mind, and will. Every day we, the lovers of Jesus, are undergoing a kind of martyrdom. By the time the fifth seal comes, there will be many overcomers crying to the Lord for His avenging. Their cry to the Lord will usher in the sixth seal, which will be the very beginning of the great tribulation.

B. The Man-child Born of the Universal Woman

The second category of overcomers will be the man-child born of the universal woman (Rev. 12:1-5). The universal woman is the totality of God's people. Out of God's people, the man-child will be born. The man-child comprises the martyrs who cry at the fifth seal and the additional martyrs before the great tribulation. There is a short time from the fifth seal to the beginning of the great tribulation. But even within such a short time, there will be a number of martyrs. These martyrs will be included in the man-child. Thus, the man-child is a bigger group than those who cry to the Lord at the fifth seal. The man-child will be resurrected and raptured to the throne of God before the three and a half years of the great tribulation (vv. 4b-6).

C. The One Hundred Forty-four Thousand Living Overcomers

Revelation 14:1-5 speaks of the one hundred forty-four thousand living overcomers raptured before the great tribulation to Mount Zion in the heavens before God's throne as firstfruits to God and to the Lamb (Rev. 14:1-5). The man-child will be the dead, martyred overcomers who will be resurrected and raptured to the throne before the great tribulation. The firstfruits to God and to the Lamb will be the living overcomers, who no doubt live a suffering life under the crucifixion of Christ, by the death of Christ. Before the great tribulation, they also will be raptured. They will not need to be resurrected, because they will have never died. All the resurrected martyred overcomers and the living overcomers will be raptured to the third heaven before the great tribulation to enjoy the Lord as the morning star (Rev. 2:28). At His second appearing Christ will be the morning star to His overcomers who watch for His coming. To all the others He will appear only as the sun (Mal. 4:2).

D. The Martyrs in the Great Tribulation

Revelation 15 speaks of the martyrs in the great tribulation under the persecution of Antichrist resurrected and raptured to stand on the glassy sea close to the end of the great tribulation (vv. 2-4; 13:7a). The glassy sea mingled with fire is a sign of the lake of fire, so these martyrs stand above the lake of fire. These are the late overcomers who will pass through the great tribulation and overcome Antichrist and the worshipping of Antichrist. They will be martyred under the persecution of Antichrist and then resurrected to reign with Christ in the millennium (20:4).

When the man-child and the firstfruits are raptured to the third heaven, many believers will be left on this earth because they have not matured. This indicates that they lived a life with very little growth in Christ, so they will be left on earth to pass through the great tribulation. That will be their trial, their test, and that will help them to give up the world. Suppose a brother loves the Lord, yet he still loves the world. When the great tribulation comes and the overcomers are raptured, will such a brother still love the world? He may cry out, "Lord Jesus, why did You leave me here? Brother So-and-so who was serving with me for years has been raptured, but I am still here." Surely this brother will repent to the Lord, turning to the Lord in a desperate way. He will not want to be left on earth until the last day of the great tribulation. This will issue in his maturity.

The resurrection and rapture of the majority of the saints will be very close to the end of the great tribulation. Even some of them will receive a reward because they will get matured through the great tribulation. After this rapture, the Lord will set up His judgment seat in the air to judge all the believers (2 Cor. 5:10). The believers either will be rewarded with the kingdom for one thousand years or will enter into outer darkness to suffer some discipline (Matt. 25:21, 23, 30).

E. The Two Witnesses Martyred, Resurrected, and Raptured to the Heavens in the Cloud at the Close of the Great Tribulation

Revelation 11:3-12 shows us the two witnesses, who will be martyred, resurrected, and raptured to the heavens in the cloud at the close of the great tribulation. These two will be

Moses and Elijah, God's living witnesses. Moses, representing the law, and Elijah, representing the prophets, both testified for God. They will be martyred by Antichrist, and their corpses will be on the street for three and a half days. Then they will be resurrected and raptured in the eyes of all their persecutors. As the overcomers, the two witnesses will be rewarded and will be in the kingdom. Moses and Elijah appeared before the Lord on the mount of transfiguration (Matt. 17:1-3). That was a miniature of the manifestation of the kingdom.

We can see from our fellowship that the overcomers are those who live the life of a martyr. To be martyred is glorious. During the Boxer Rebellion in China in the early 1900s, many Christians were martyred. One man told me the story of a young girl who was martyred during this time. He was working one day when the Boxers were parading on the street with their long swords in a threatening way. He looked through a crack in the door and saw them leading a young Christian girl to her death. Instead of being frightened, she was singing and praising. When this man saw her, he was shocked and said to himself that there must be something special about being a Christian. Because of this, he sought to find out what this "foreign religion" of being a Christian was, and he was saved by the Lord. Actually, he was saved through that young martyr. Later, he gave up his business and became a traveling preacher. When I was in Chefoo, he told me this story of how he was saved and became a minister of Christ. This young martyr, through whom he was saved, was a real overcomer.

II. THE FINAL CONSUMMATION OF THE OVERCOMERS

Now we want to see the final consummation of the overcomers. We need to see what the overcomers consummate and accomplish.

A. To Be Manifested as a Corporate Overcomer after Their Raptures

Eventually, all of the overcomers will be manifested as a corporate overcomer after their raptures. After they are raptured, they all become one entity. They are really built together. This can be proved by two things. First, all the overcomers become one bride to Christ (Rev. 19:7-9). Christ will not have many brides, but only one bride, who is constituted with all the overcomers. This is proof that all the overcomers will become one. Second, they become the heavenly army to follow Christ to defeat Antichrist and those who follow him (vv. 11-21). All the overcomers first become the bride, and after her marriage to Christ, the bride becomes the army. All the overcomers are really one.

This means that today, in this age before the rapture, we have to learn the lesson of how to be one and of how to coordinate with one another with no opinion. We should reject our opinion and care only for our growth in Christ, transformation in Christ, and building up in Christ. If we are such persons, the church life will be pleasant to us. When we are right persons, everything is right and pleasant to us. But when we are wrong persons, we are unhappy and everything is wrong and unpleasant to us. When we are right in an overcoming situation, we love everything and everyone, and every situation is no problem to us. Today in the church life, those who condemn and criticize others are the wrong persons. If someone comes to us to say something negative about the church, about the elders, about the ministry, about the brothers, or about the sisters, we have to realize that this person is a wrong person. We should stay away from such persons (Rom. 16:17). Otherwise, we will be contaminated. In this age we have to learn the lesson to coordinate with all the lovers of Christ. Then after our rapture, we will be ready to go along with one another, and will be one entity as Christ's bride and Christ's army.

B. To Be Rewarded
at the Judgment Seat of Christ

The overcomers will be rewarded at the judgment seat of Christ (2 Cor. 5:10; Rev. 11:18c). Christ will judge His believers not concerning their eternal salvation but concerning their dispensational reward (1 Cor. 4:4-5; 3:13-15).

C. To Be the Bride Married to the Lamb

The overcomers will also be the bride married to the Lamb (Rev. 19:7-9).

D. To Be the Army of the Lamb

They will also be the army of the Lamb (Rev. 17:14; 19:14). According to Joel 3:11, they will come as the mighty ones with Christ to defeat Antichrist and his armies (Rev. 19:19-21) to close the great tribulation and the present age. We should not be those who love this age, because we need to become the ones to close it. The overcomers will come with Christ to close this present, evil, and ugly age. We can hasten the Lord's coming and the closing of this age by being the overcomers to stand against the tide and the trend of the entire situation and environment on this earth.

E. To Bring in the Kingdom of God and of Christ

When we close the great tribulation and this age, we will bring in the kingdom of God and of Christ (Rev. 11:15; 20:4, 6). The kingdom will not come spontaneously by itself. The kingdom will come by our bringing it in.

F. To Inherit the Kingdom of God and of Christ in the Fuller Enjoyment of the Eternal Life

The overcomers will inherit the kingdom of God and of Christ in the fuller enjoyment of the eternal life (Matt. 5:20; 19:23-30; 1 Cor. 6:9-10; Gal. 5:19-21; Eph. 5:3-5; 2 Pet. 1:11). First, they bring in the kingdom, and then they inherit it. They will be the co-kings with Christ (Rev. 20:4, 6; Matt. 19:28). Christ will be the leader of the kings, and the overcomers will be the co-kings to co-reign with Christ. The overcomers will also be priests of God and of Christ in the millennium (Rev. 20:6; 22:3b) to enjoy the ruling authority over the nations (Rev. 2:26-27; 12:5). To man, the overcomers will be the kings. To God and to Christ, they will be the priests. What a blessing!

G. To Be the New Jerusalem,
as the Bride of Christ
for One Thousand Years,
in Its Initial and Fresh Stage

What God wants is the New Jerusalem, which will be the totality of what the overcomers are. Eventually, all the overcomers will be the New Jerusalem, as the bride of Christ for one thousand years, in its initial and fresh stage. These one thousand years will be counted as one day (2 Pet. 3:8), the wedding day. This will be the initial and fresh stage of the New Jerusalem as the bride of Christ.

The overcomers will also be the New Jerusalem as the present Paradise of God in the millennial kingdom (Rev. 2:7). This bride will be the Paradise of God. The three things are one: the bride, the city, and the Paradise of God.

The overcomers will shine forth like the sun in the kingdom of their Father in the heavenly part of the millennium (Matt. 13:43; cf. Dan. 12:2-3, 13). The millennium will have two parts: the heavenly part and the earthly part. The saved Israelites who will repent at the Lord's coming back (Rom. 11:26-27; Zech. 12:10; Ezek. 36:25-28) will be the priests in the earthly part (Zech. 8:20-23; Isa. 2:2-3), which will be the kingdom of the Son of Man (Matt. 13:41; Rev. 11:15); whereas the overcoming believers will be in the heavenly part to shine as the sun in the kingdom of their Father. For one thousand years, the overcomers will shine forth the light, and the light is the Triune God Himself (1 John 1:5).

H. To Consummate and Complete
the New Jerusalem in Full, as
the Tabernacle of God and the Wife of Christ
in the New Heaven and New Earth for Eternity

Eventually, the New Jerusalem will be consummated and completed in full, as the tabernacle of God and the wife of Christ in the new heaven and new earth for eternity (Rev. 21:1-3, 9-10). In the kingdom of one thousand years, the New Jerusalem will be composed only of the overcomers. Besides the overcomers there will be a great number of immature saints, but after the thousand-year kingdom, all the believers will be matured. The Lord has a way to cause all the believers to be matured. If we do not get matured in this age, we will be matured in the next age. The process of being matured in the next age, however, will be very severe. Eventually, all of the believers will join the overcomers to make the New Jerusalem larger than it was in the thousand-year kingdom. That will consummate and complete the New Jerusalem in full, as the tabernacle of God and the wife of Christ in the new heaven and new earth for eternity.

In eternity the New Jerusalem will be the wife of Christ. On the wedding day, the wife is the bride, but after the wedding day she is no longer the bride but simply the wife. The believers who do not overcome in this age will participate in the New Jerusalem as the wife, but they will have no share in her as the bride because they will mature too late. The New Jerusalem in eternity future will be with the addition of all the saints perfected for their maturity in the divine life through the discipline in the kingdom age (Rev. 21:2, 12, 14). This will be for the eternal expression, to its fullest extent, of the processed Triune God in, with, and through all the regenerated, transformed, and glorified tripartite saints in eternity (Rev. 21:10-11).

I. To Consummate Finally
the Triune God's Eternal Economy
in Christ through the Consummated Spirit

The overcomers will consummate finally the Triune God's eternal economy in Christ through the consummated Spirit. This is proven by Revelation 22:17—"The Spirit and the bride say, Come!" The bride is the overcomers, and the Spirit is the consummated Triune God. This is the ultimate consummation of the entire economy of God, and this consummation is the glorified saints married to the processed and consummated Triune God.

J. To Participate in the Fullest Enjoyment
of the Processed and Consummated Triune God

The overcomers will participate in the fullest enjoyment of

the processed and consummated Triune God in the fellowship with all the redeemed and glorified saints forever and ever. In the thousand-year kingdom, the overcomers will be happy, but they will no doubt miss their spiritual relatives, the other brothers and sisters in Christ. But after the one thousand years, all the believers will be matured to be included with the overcomers as the New Jerusalem for eternity. Then we will enjoy the Triune God in fellowship with all the saints throughout the ages as the New Jerusalem forever to be in His glory as His expression for His satisfaction. In this chapter we have seen the New Jerusalem. Our "dream" is to become the New Jerusalem as the final consummation of the overcomers and the consummation of God's economy.

A CONCLUDING WORD

In the universal scene, there are mainly two persons—God and man. There are millions of other lifeless and organic things, which may be considered as a decoration to God's universe. God loves beauty because He is a God of beauty. The living creatures and the plant life are beautiful. God did not create an empty heaven and a barren earth but a universe of beauty. All the items of beauty in the universe created by God may be considered as God's decoration, but the main things in the universe are two persons—God and man.

If you take God and man away, the entire universe will have no real history. The universe has a history, beginning with the creation of man, of approximately six thousand years. The real history of the entire universe is concerning God *with* man and concerning God *within* man. The Old Testament, from Genesis through Malachi is the history of God *with* man. Genesis 1 says that God created man, and Malachi 4 says that God will come to man as the Sun of righteousness with healing in His wings (v. 2). Sun dispels all the darkness, and healing swallows up all our sickness. In the age of restoration we will have the unique God as our Sun and our healing. Everything will be restored by His healing and by His shining. When He shines and heals, we are restored.

The history of the entire universe is a history of God with

man in the Old Testament, but this is not the ultimate consummation. Still, we have the New Testament. In the New Testament we see a further history of God. Now this God is not just with man; He is *within* man. The first chapter of Matthew tells us how He got into man. He was conceived in the womb of a virgin. He was the Creator, who could call things into being. In the old creation, He spoke things into being. When He said, "Let there be light," there was light (Gen. 1:3). This is the way He creates. But in the New Testament, He was conceived in the womb of a virgin and remained there for nine months.

Matthew 1:20 says, "That which has been begotten in her is of the Holy Spirit." God was born into Mary through His Spirit. That which was born in Mary was God. God was born there, and He remained there exactly nine months. This was surely a great step. When He created the universe, He spent only six days. But for Him to enter into man was not a simple matter. To enter into man means to join with man and to be one with man.

God has the divine life, the uncreated life, and man has the human life, the created life. How could these two lives be together as one, and how could there be a living of these two lives as one living? This is why God entered into man. He was divine yet He was born human. No one can exhaust the study of this wonderful One. Who is He? He is God, but He is more than God. He is also man. He is the complete God and the perfect man. We have to call Him the God-man. The term *God-man* implies so much. This One who is our God, our Savior, our Redeemer, our Lord, and our Master is marvelous and far beyond our natural comprehension.

In Matthew 1 we can see how the unique God became a man. His name was *Emmanuel,* meaning *God with us* (v. 23). He was God with man. Then He lived on this earth, and He died a wonderful, vicarious, all-inclusive death to terminate every negative thing in the universe. His death was also a life-releasing death. In His death, He released Himself out of the human shell which He had put on. His resurrection was a life-imparting resurrection. In resurrection He became a life-giving Spirit (1 Cor. 15:45b) to take a second step to enter into man.

In the first step of incarnation He entered into man with the divine essence, to bring God into man, but through the second step of resurrection, He enters into man with two essences, the divine essence and the human essence. A divine-human mingled essence enters into man. When He entered into us in the second step, all the aspects of His person and work were included. When He entered into us, the complete God and the perfect man entered with His human living, crucifixion, resurrection, and ascension. When we were born of our human parents, we did not realize all the things that we received genetically. In the same principle, when we were regenerated, when God came into us, we did not realize that many wonderful things came into us. When we give Christ the first place, taking Him as our first love, we grow in Him. It is by our growth in life that we begin to realize what we have inherited by our divine birth.

In the process of living the Christian life, I have discovered many things, not just by my own experiences but also by the revelation in the Holy Bible. In God's economy there are three crucial factors—God and man plus the Bible, which reveals the history of God in His union with man. In the Bible we have seen that the unique God desires to be wrought into man, making Himself one with man. He lives in this man and this man lives in Him. These two entities have one living.

The apostle Paul said that our outer man is being consumed, but our inner man is being renewed day by day (2 Cor. 4:16). To be consumed means to be reduced and to be renewed means to be increased. The old man is decaying, reducing, and the new man is increasing. Our inner man is being renewed with God. This means that the very Triune God is working Himself into us. If we are willing to receive His working, to say "yes" to His working, we will be the overcomers.

The overcomers enjoy God in them to be their grace for their enjoyment. The result, the coming out, is the Triune God wrought into and mingled with our tripartite being to make us one person, one entity. The New Jerusalem, which is the totality of all the overcomers, is a divine mingling of the processed Triune God with the redeemed and transformed tripartite man, a mingling of divinity with humanity, issuing in a universal, corporate, mysterious person. This is the conclusion of the entire Bible and of the history of God, first *with* man and second *within* man.

In the entire universe, the crucial items are God plus man plus His divine revelation, which is the Bible. At the conclusion of the divine revelation, all of God's chosen and redeemed people will be absolutely one in the Triune God. He is three but He is uniquely one, so in the Triune God, the three-one God, we all can be made one. The conclusion of the divine revelation is the New Jerusalem, which is the processed, consummated Triune God wrought into our tripartite, God-created being, making the Triune God and us one entity.

ABOUT THE AUTHOR

Witness Lee was born in 1905 in northern China and raised in a Christian family. At age nineteen he was fully captured for Christ and immediately consecrated himself to preach the gospel for the rest of his life. Early in his service, he met Watchman Nee, a renowned preacher, teacher, and writer. Witness Lee labored together with Watchman Nee under his direction. In 1934 Watchman Nee entrusted Witness Lee with the responsibility for his publication operation, called the Shanghai Gospel Book Room.

Prior to the Communist takeover in 1949, Witness Lee was sent by Watchman Nee and his other co-workers to Taiwan to ensure that the things delivered to them by the Lord would not be lost. Watchman Nee instructed Witness Lee to continue the former's publishing operation abroad as the Taiwan Gospel Book Room, which has been publicly recognized as the publisher of Watchman Nee's works outside China. Witness Lee's work in Taiwan manifested the Lord's abundant blessing. From a mere three hundred fifty believers, newly fled from the mainland, the churches in Taiwan grew to twenty thousand believers in five years.

In 1962 Witness Lee felt led of the Lord to move to the United States, and he began to minister in Los Angeles in December of that year. During his thirty-five years of service throughout the United States, he ministered in weekly meetings, weekend conferences, and weeklong trainings, delivering several thousand spoken messages. His speaking has since been published, and many of his books have been translated into numerous languages. He gave his last public conference in February 1997 at the age of ninety-one and went to be with the Lord, whom he loved and served, on June 9, 1997. Witness Lee leaves behind a prolific presentation of the truth in the Bible. His major work, *Life-study of the Bible,* the fruit of his labor from 1974 to 1995, comprises over twenty-five thousand pages of commentary on every book of the Bible from the perspective of the believers' enjoyment and experience of God's divine life in Christ through the Holy Spirit. In addition, *The Collected Works of Witness Lee* contains over one hundred thirty volumes (over seventy-five thousand pages) of his other ministry from 1932 to 1997. Witness Lee was also the chief editor of a new translation of the New Testament into Chinese called the Recovery Version, and he directed the translation of the English New Testament Recovery Version. The Recovery Version also appears in over twenty-five other languages. In the Recovery Version he provided an extensive body of footnotes, outlines, and spiritual cross references. A radio broadcast of his messages can be heard on Christian radio stations in the United States and Europe. In 1965 Witness Lee founded Living Stream Ministry, a non-profit corporation, located in Anaheim, California, which publishes his and Watchman Nee's ministry.

Witness Lee's ministry emphasizes the experience of Christ as life and the practical oneness of the believers as the Body of Christ. Stressing the importance of attending to both of these matters, he led the churches under his care to grow in Christian life and function. He was unbending in his conviction that God's goal is not narrow sectarianism but the universal Body of Christ. In time, believers everywhere began to meet simply as the church in their localities in response to this conviction. Through his ministry hundreds of local churches have been raised up throughout the earth.

OTHER BOOKS PUBLISHED BY
Living Stream Ministry

Titles by Witness Lee:

Abraham—Called by God	978-0-7363-0359-0
The Experience of Life	978-0-87083-417-2
The Knowledge of Life	978-0-87083-419-6
The Tree of Life	978-0-87083-300-7
The Economy of God	978-0-87083-415-8
The Divine Economy	978-0-87083-268-0
God's New Testament Economy	978-0-87083-199-7
The World Situation and God's Move	978-0-87083-092-1
Christ vs. Religion	978-0-87083-010-5
The All-inclusive Christ	978-0-87083-020-4
Gospel Outlines	978-0-87083-039-6
Character	978-0-87083-322-9
The Secret of Experiencing Christ	978-0-87083-227-7
The Life and Way for the Practice of the Church Life	978-0-87083-785-2
The Basic Revelation in the Holy Scriptures	978-0-87083-105-8
The Crucial Revelation of Life in the Scriptures	978-0-87083-372-4
The Spirit with Our Spirit	978-0-87083-798-2
Christ as the Reality	978-0-87083-047-1
The Central Line of the Divine Revelation	978-0-87083-960-3
The Full Knowledge of the Word of God	978-0-87083-289-5
Watchman Nee—A Seer of the Divine Revelation ...	978-0-87083-625-1

Titles by Watchman Nee:

How to Study the Bible	978-0-7363-0407-8
God's Overcomers	978-0-7363-0433-7
The New Covenant	978-0-7363-0088-9
The Spiritual Man • 3 volumes	978-0-7363-0269-2
Authority and Submission	978-0-7363-0185-5
The Overcoming Life	978-1-57593-817-2
The Glorious Church	978-0-87083-745-6
The Prayer Ministry of the Church	978-0-87083-860-6
The Breaking of the Outer Man and the Release ...	978-1-57593-955-1
The Mystery of Christ	978-1-57593-954-4
The God of Abraham, Isaac, and Jacob	978-0-87083-932-0
The Song of Songs	978-0-87083-872-9
The Gospel of God • 2 volumes	978-1-57593-953-7
The Normal Christian Church Life	978-0-87083-027-3
The Character of the Lord's Worker	978-1-57593-322-1
The Normal Christian Faith	978-0-87083-748-7
Watchman Nee's Testimony	978-0-87083-051-8

Available at
Christian bookstores, or contact Living Stream Ministry
2431 W. La Palma Ave. • Anaheim, CA 92801
1-800-549-5164 • www.livingstream.com